# VISUALISATION
## AN INTRODUCTORY GUIDE

# VISUALISATION
## AN INTRODUCTORY GUIDE

Use visualisation to improve your
health and develop your
self-awareness and creativity

# HELEN GRAHAM

PIATKUS

© 1996 Helen Graham

First published in 1996 by
Judy Piatkus (Publishers) Ltd
5 Windmill Street, London W1P 1HF

The moral right of the author has been asserted

A catalogue record for this book is available
from the British Library
ISBN 0-7499-1652-4

Edited by Carol Franklin
Designed by Sue Ryall

Set in Sabon by Action Typesetting, Gloucester

Printed in Great Britain by
Biddles Ltd, Guildford & King's Lynn

# CONTENTS

# INTRODUCTION

The letter from Mike read quite simply 'I want to learn how to use visualisation. I would be grateful if you could put me in touch with someone who can help me'. I replied to the effect that I would be willing to help him. On this basis we arranged to meet. When we did it was clear that Mike was very ill indeed. His face was pale and almost translucent, and like his head totally hairless. His eyes, curiously accentuated by the lack of eyebrows, showed pain. His handshake was weak, and he removed his coat and sat down with difficulty. Aged just 31 he had recently been told by his doctors that there was nothing more they could do for him.

Mike didn't want to die, so in desperation he was pursuing any form of treatment that offered him hope of recovery. He had been excited to learn that visualisation has proved effective in the treatment of cancer and that many cancer sufferers have attributed their recovery either wholly or in part to it. However, upon attending an 'alternative' cancer care centre he had been devastated to discover that he could not 'do' the visualisation exercises recommended there. Try as he might – and he assured me he had tried very hard – he could not produce visual images. This experience had left him with feelings of failure and inadequacy. He concluded that he simply hadn't the ability to visualise, and that it might be pointless for him to continue trying.

Mike wanted me to tell him whether or not he could 'learn' visualisation. I didn't give a straightforward answer. Instead I asked him what he meant by visualisation and why he thought he needed to learn it. He replied, 'It's imagining, and I'm not very imaginative' – a self-assessment reinforced by his experience at the cancer care centre.

I pointed out that his ideas about visualisation were only partly correct. Visualisation *is* imagining; producing mental images that come to mind as pictures we can 'see'. However, images may also be sensed in other ways – as sounds, smells, feelings or impressions of various kinds, so visualisation is only one aspect of imagining, although for most people it is the most important. The ability to imagine how things look, sound, smell, taste and feel when they are not immediately present is so commonplace that most people don't recognise it as an ability at all, and don't consider themselves to be imaginative – believing that only artists and other creative people possess this specialised talent. Undoubtedly some people are more imaginative than others, just as some people are better footballers than others. In the same way, some people rely more on visual images than other sense impressions. Nevertheless almost everybody produces visual images, and most underestimate the extent to which they rely on them in everyday life.

I explained to Mike that trying is totally counterproductive because mental images emerge most easily in dreams, day-dreams, fantasy and reverie, when we are relaxed. Trying involves effort, or mental and physical exertion, whereas relaxation is a lessening of effort and exertion, or rest. Images are most likely to emerge when we give up trying and let go of the mental and physical tensions.

Mike could easily accept this. He recalled that as a child he had spent much time absorbed in the visual images of fantasy, day-dreaming and play, and that as he got older he was often criticised by his parents and teachers for being 'idle' instead of applying himself to activities such as reading, writing and arithmetic. Gradually he had spent less and less time engaged in imagining. He acknowledged that now, as an adult, he applied himself more to the intellectual activities he had neglected in his youth and was rarely relaxed. Now with a university degree, he couldn't understand why he found visualisation so difficult. Perhaps, he reasoned, visualisation might not 'work' for him anyway?

I explained to Mike that visualisation often enables us to confront and overcome fears and anxieties, discover features of ourselves of which formerly we were fully or partly unaware, become aware of the attitudes and beliefs that shape our lives and govern our thoughts, feelings and behaviour, and so reassess ourselves and our lives. It can help us define what we want from life, or equally important, what we don't want. Visualisation may also enable us to recognise the ways in which we prevent ourselves from realising our ambitions and dreams. Frequently it highlights our failure to seize and make the most of opportunities presented to us, and enables us to see what can happen to us when we suffer from doubts, poor self-esteem, negativity, anxiety or guilt. Visualisation can help us to explore personal needs and potentials that are often unconscious, unacknowledged and confused. By exploring personal images and the symbols inherent in them we can learn how to establish contact with previously unrecognised aspects of ourselves, integrate these aspects and heal ourselves in the true sense of the word. Visualisation can therefore not only be life-changing but life-enhancing. It can 'work' for anyone.

As I finished speaking I noticed that Mike was smiling. He said 'While you were talking I suddenly had an image of where I stand at present'.

'Where's that?', I asked.

'On a staircase', he replied.

'Going up or down?'

'Neither', he said. 'I can see myself facing the stair rail. I can't see anything beyond. It's all black. All I know is I'm very afraid, and holding on to the stair rail for dear life'.

In this way, quite spontaneously, without trying and with his eyes wide open, Mike realised not only that he was capable of visualisation but also that the image he had produced gave profound insight into his situation and feelings, enabling him fully to acknowledge these for the first time.

So began Mike's exploration of himself by way of visualisation. He had started a journey of self-discovery, self-growth and development in the course of which he reappraised himself and his life, and as a result broke off several stressful relationships, moved home, made new friends, found a new girlfriend, took up sculpture, music and language lessons and travelled abroad. His cancer went into remission; his primary tumour regressed and a couple of secondary tumours disappeared.

# The Steps To Beginning Visualisation

This book explains how visualisation can bring about self-discovery, self-growth and development; how it can be used to make positive changes in your life, and relieve physical symptoms and pain. It sets out and explains the steps you can take in beginning visualisation. Chapter 1 explains how visualisation works and its many uses. Chapter 2 tells you how to begin visualisation; how to overcome initial difficulties and make progress, and how to understand your images. In chapters 3–9 there are exercises which show you how use visualisation for relaxation, to manage stress, develop greater self-awareness, realise your dreams, treat symptoms of disease, manage pain and develop spiritually. The comments of many people who have used these exercises to begin visualisation are included in the chapters. A guide to further reading can be found at the end of the book.

# 1

## WHAT IS VISUALISATION?

*The possible's slow fuse
is lit by the imagination.*
Emily Dickinson

### Seeing In The Mind's Eye

Visualisation is thinking in pictures as opposed to words. We all have the ability to make pictures or images in the mind – to 'see in the mind's eye'. This ability is a function of the lower, older and more primitive parts of the brain, but just as during evolution the parts of the brain that produce visual images have been overlaid by those responsible for verbal language, so thinking in words has also obscured our everyday reliance on visual images. Many of us only become aware of these when the verbal chatter in our mind is temporarily suspended or reduced. This occurs spontaneously in dreams, during fantasy, day-dreaming and reverie, and deliberately during meditation, hypnosis, biofeedback, autogenic training (see p. 105) and creative visualisation – that is, in circumstances where we relax and stop thinking in words. Some people insist that they don't produce visual images. However, it may be truer to say that words so dominate their thinking that they don't attend to visual images and as a result are not aware of them. For these people, visual imagery can be said to be largely 'unconscious'.

## Everyday Uses Of Visual Images

Everyone – except those with certain kinds of brain damage – generates visual images, and everyone bases choices and decisions on them. Take, for example, ordinary, everyday decisions. How do you decide what clothes to wear? You probably picture in your mind's eye how the different garments will look together and how you will look in them. Perhaps you also imagine the weather for the day ahead and the places in which you are likely to be. We tend to picture features of our environment in much the same way and this enables us to coordinate furnishings, fittings and the decor of our homes, work and leisure places. Without the ability to do this we would never be able to create or 'read' plans for buildings or to lay out parks and gardens. We would find it difficult to plan meals or to choose our holiday destinations. The mental pictures we summon about Santorini, Seattle or Skegness enable us to decide whether or not we wish to go there. More fundamentally, this ability enables us to picture ourselves, our past, present and future. We all rely on our ability to think in pictures to a far greater extent than we may at first appreciate.

This oversight is not merely individual but cultural. Western culture in particular emphasises the importance of verbal thought and of the spoken and written word. The way we use language distinguishes us from animals.

Thinking in words enables us to reason, rationalise, separate and categorise – activities that have made human progress and development possible, especially scientific and technological development. But this emphasis on the importance of language has tended to obscure some of its shortcomings and limitations.

## The Limitations Of Language

Many naturally non-verbal issues cannot easily be conceived or expressed in words. This is true of most physical, physiological, psychological and emotional processes. It is difficult to think about many aspects of ordinary life, including health and illness, happiness, hardship and other feelings in words. The singer-songwriter Suzanne Vega conveys the difficulty in her song *Solitude Standing*:

> *Words are too solid*
> *They don't move fast enough,*
> *To catch the blur in the brain*
> *That flies and is gone ...*
> *They don't mean what I meant*
> *They don't say what I said*
> *They're just the crust of the meaning*
> *With realms underneath*
> *Never touched*
> *Never stirred*
> *Never even moved through.*

The limitations of words in describing personal experience can easily be demonstrated in relation to pain. This is an almost universal experience. Only a tiny minority of people are born without pain receptors; the rest of us all experience pain. If you are asked to think about pain you are likely to bring to mind a situation in which it occurred, whether at the dentist, during childbirth, in a car accident and so on. If you are then asked to describe your pain you will probably find that you have to resort to metaphors. You may describe the pain feeling like being stabbed, shot, burned, stung or squeezed. These are essentially visual rather than bodily images because as anyone knows who has been unexpectedly stabbed or shot there is, initially at least, no sensation of pain. Many people who are stabbed or shot don't realise they have been, which is why soldiers with dreadful wounds can continue in battle and why people who have had limbs severed can often carry them and go in search of help. Not only the quality of pain experience eludes language but also the quantity. Most of us are obliged to resort to 'it hurts a lot' or 'a little' to convey our degree of suffering.

## Emotional Expression

It is even more difficult to describe emotional experiences in words. Think about your positive feelings. The entire range and complexity of these tend to be expressed with the verbs 'like' and 'love'. There isn't much in between. Some of us favour one end of the scale and will say 'Oh yes, I like him a lot' or 'I'd really like to win the lottery'; whereas others say they 'love' everything from McDonald's fries, the colour green, Mel Gibson, Tina Turner, Benidorm, their mother and God. The same word covers a range of emotions from the sublime to the ridiculous.

The number of words for a particular thing in a

language reflects the value placed on it within that culture. The Inuit have many words for snow and Arabs distinguish camels of many kinds. The lack of words for emotions in the English language reflects the fact that our culture, and Western culture as a whole, places a relatively low value on feelings as opposed to intellect. This can lead to problems, especially in relationships, because we can't adequately express our feelings or convey them to others.

Our lack of words for emotions has even greater implications for our inner dialogue because we have very few ways of representing our emotions to ourselves. We often have strong feelings but no means of making sense of them. So to defend ourselves against unpleasant feelings we frequently rationalise them, and in doing so hope to explain them away. But these explanations don't remove the feelings or help us deal with them. In order to cope with emotional problems, and with some physical ones, we need to be able to explore and express our feelings rather than rationalise and dismiss them, and this usually proves difficult because we very quickly run out of words. When this happens we are obliged to resort to metaphor to convey our feelings: 'I feel like a bottle of pop ready to explode'; 'I feel as though a ton of bricks has fallen on me'; 'I feel exposed to the core'. These images help because they enable us to represent our feelings visually. They are often very effective in promoting greater self-awareness or insight, and show us more about our attitude to a particular situation or to life in general. By giving expression to feelings that may otherwise be repressed, visualisation can contribute greatly to our emotional well-being.

# Problem Solving

Visualisation also has an important intellectual role. Thinking in words may impede decision making and problem solving, and limit coping strategies. Think about the following problem devised by Duncker in 1945:

> *One morning at sunrise a Buddhist monk began to climb a mountain on a narrow path that wound around it. He climbed at a steady 3 miles per hour. After 12 hours he reached the top where there was a temple and remained there to meditate for several days. Then at sunrise he started down the same path, walking at a steady 5 miles per hour. Prove that there must be a spot along the same path which he occupied on both trips at exactly the same time of day.*

Applying verbal reasoning and logic to this problem is unhelpful. Indeed the more intellectual you are and the more developed your capacity for rational thinking and logic the less likely you are to solve it. A less sophisticated person might quickly 'see' the solution to the problem. Certainly representing it visually is far more efficient, as Duncker shows:

> *Imagine a monk climbing a mountain in the course of a day. Imagine also a second monk descending the mountain in the course of a day. Now superimpose the two images as if the two journeys were undertaken on the same day. Clearly at some point during the day the monks must meet and therefore be at the same point at the same time. This holds equally true for the case of a single monk making the two journeys on separate days.*

'Seeing' solutions to problems in this way is a very different technique from verbal reasoning. Because our culture and education system favour verbal thinking most of us don't value, use or fully develop our imaginative capacities. We tend only to bring part of our mind to bear on issues that could be quickly and effectively resolved by using visualisation.

## The Key To Creativity

The ability to think in pictures provides us with an important tool for acquiring and processing knowledge. It gives us, quite literally, a different way of looking at our lives. The most important scientific thinkers of the twentieth century have relied more on their imaginative abilities than on verbal reasoning. Albert Einstein claimed that he had no special talent other than his ability to visualise. The experiments which formed the basis of quantum physics were conducted in his head rather than a laboratory and hence are referred to as *gedanken* or thought experiments. Scientists such as Faraday, Clerk Maxwell, Kekule, Eddington, Planck, Schroedinger, Heisenberg and Feynman also relied heavily on imagination in the formulation of their theories, as have many distinguished mathematicians.

When combined with verbal reasoning visualisation increases the flexibility of our mental processes and greatly enhances our mental capabilities. The ability to 'see' the nature of reality and solutions to problems in this way appears to be the key to all creative ability, whether in the sciences or the arts. As Goya observed, 'Fantasy abandoned by reason produces impossible monsters. United with her, she is the mother of the arts and the origin of their marvels'. This awareness has led to a great increase in research on visual imagery within psychology and allied fields and its wide application in diverse disciplines.

## 'Turning Things Over' In The Mind

Visualisation and visual perception share many features including the ways in which they are processed within the brain. The saying that 'a picture is worth a thousand words' also applies to visual images which present a great deal of complex information much more quickly than language.

Mental images also correspond in most respects to perceived or seen objects and can replace them in our minds. We can often answer questions about objects just as well when we merely imagine them as when we perceive them. We can also imagine all the perspectives which might be perceived when viewing objects from various sides or angles. We can further modify these images and obtain information from them just as we might do with corresponding physical objects and processes. We can mentally rotate imagined objects, add, subtract, superimpose or otherwise change their features, and move them around in various ways. We can indeed 'turn things over in our minds', and as a means of 'reality' testing and problem solving this is often superior to 'rational' logical strategies. In this way it is possible to imagine specific activities without taking the time, making the effort or running the risk of carrying out those activities in physical reality. It was by imagining himself travelling into space alongside a beam of light that Einstein developed his theory of relativity.

# Physiological Effects

It is an age-old belief that visual images can have direct physiological effects. We begin to salivate when we imagine eating a lemon, and it is well known that sexual or fearful imagery can produce dramatic physiological reactions. It is less widely known but just as well established that visualisation can produce changes in blood flow, blood sugar levels, gastro-intestinal activity, heart rate, blood pressure, perspiration, muscular tension, breathing, eye movement and pupil size, and the formation of blisters. Recent experimental and clinical studies have confirmed that visualisation can also affect immune functioning. The response of white blood cells and hormones to standard tests of physiological stress can be enhanced by appropriate visual images. These findings suggest that visualisation may help us to control physiological functions formerly thought to be involuntary, and to harness this ability more systematically in the treatment of illness. Heart rate can be controlled, blood pressure lowered and numerous physiological functions regulated by visual images. Long-lasting benefits can also be achieved with visualisation.

Although the way in which visualisation works is still not precisely understood it appears that images build a bridge between mind and body allowing information to cross from the psychological to the physical domain, and vice versa. Physiological information may be perceived in visual or symbolic form as images. These can provide important clues to physiological functioning and be used as a tool for accessing previously unconscious, or hidden, physiological and emotional processes. Images may offer a more immediate and direct expression of the unconscious than language as they are less likely to be filtered through the conscious rational process of censorship that words are subjected to before they assume grammatical order and can be spoken.

Physiological effects can also be induced by the psychological and emotional information conveyed in visual images. This process is known as active imagination or creative visualisation. Physiological effects may also be induced unconsciously in so far that a person may be unaware that the mental pictures he or she habitually generates in response to psychological experiences have physiological consequences. For example, if you always see yourself as likely to be threatened by others your body will constantly be alert to defend you. Your blood pressure and heart rate will be raised and your muscles will be tense.

Visualisation is highly absorbing and as with any activity which engages and occupies our attention it is also relaxing. The manner in which images form simultaneously and instantaneously in the mind results in a time sense quite unrelated to serial clock time. This relieves time-related stress in those to whom time is a pressure, and because it helps reduce reliance on verbal thinking it relieves the physical tensions that frequently arise from mental anxieties.

## Visualisation In Action

Visualisation has numerous and diverse applications, but it is only relatively recently that these have been recognised and exploited. The reason for this is that imagery was not considered a real and genuine subject for study until the early 1970s. Before then it was relegated to the world of the poets. Psychologists began to investigate the phenomenon only when it became clear that astonishing feats of memory can be accomplished with the aid of visual imagery, and that stage performers train their memory by visualisation.

Some of the growing number of uses of visualisation are listed below.

## Memory aid

One of the simplest ways of learning a list of items is to link the first and the second items together as vividly as possible with a strong visual image and then produce a further image to link a third item, and so on. This method of 'chaining' can be used for items other than words so that a sequence of ideas and actions can be memorised.

Another way of committing to memory a list of items or succession of ideas is to imagine a familiar place such as a street and assign certain images to successive landmarks. These can later be recalled by imagining the place and visualising the items associated with each landmark. In this way visual images function as powerful aids to memory and learning.

## Creative management

Increasingly visualisation is being used to stimulate creative thinking and to train decision making and problem solving skills by business and management consultants. Visualisation is at the heart of creative management. It can be used in training people in the art of managing change, and in developing new ways of thinking about organisation and management. It is impossible to develop new styles of organisation and management while continuing to think in old ways. What Gareth Morgan calls 'imaginization' in his book of the same title (see Bibliography) is an invitation to reimage ourselves and what we do:

*This ability to invent evocative images or stories that can resonate with the challenges at hand and help motivate and mobilize people to achieve desired goals, or to cope with the unknown, is becoming a key managerial skill. It is central to the process of imaginization.*

## Selling techniques

Visualisation techniques are also being exploited in the commercial field. They are used in advertising and market research to explore unconscious associations to advertised products including medicines. The packaging of products relies heavily on visual images derived from this kind of research. In the field of public relations, subjects' responses to public figures such as politicians, as revealed through visual images, are used as the basis for impression management and image building.

## Planning and performance

In all fields involving planning, design and research visualisation is used implicitly as projects are envisioned in the mind's eye before being put to the test. By going through the motions of what you do or plan to do in the mind you can see possible flaws in performance or planning and avoid them. You can anticipate problems and ways of overcoming them. Just as works of literature and scientific experiments can be prepared in the mind before being embodied, mentally rehearsing an activity and its effects is well documented among sportspersons who mentally run through every part of a race or competition beforehand in order to overcome anxieties and self-doubts, cope with problems and raise the level of their performance. The former athlete David Jenkins attributed his failure to add an Olympic gold medal to his many other sporting achievements to his inability to 'see' it happen. Olympic gold medallist David Hemery has suggested that 'perhaps what is needed to achieve something more, something greater than ourselves, is to have vision beyond ourselves' (see Bibliography).

Visualisation is increasingly being advocated as a necessary feature of training by sports psychologists. In some cases visualisation may substitute for actual training experience. The British bobsleigh team at the 1994 Winter Olympics used this method in training in lieu of actual practice on the slopes.

Mental rehearsal by way of visualisation is also widely employed by actors, dancers and musicians as a way to enhance artistic and musical performance.

## Coping skills

Because visualisation is absorbing and therefore relaxing it is being used as an aid to relaxation, stress management and coping skills in industry, business and commerce, and in assertiveness training. The tension-reducing features of visualisation are also being applied to assist in classroom control and management, and to help children cope with potentially stressful situations such as examinations.

Visualisation is a valuable way to access and express issues which may be difficult for individuals, especially children, to articulate – issues such as abuse, phobias, bullying, emotional and physical pain. It is being used increasingly in social work and by educational psychologists. Visualisation can also give parents insight into the normally hidden realms of their children's experiences (their fears, anxieties, needs, wishes and preoccupations) and help them monitor their emotional and psychological development more sensitively. Certainly, to the extent that visualisation helps us to explore our inner worlds it can help us to become more sensitive to the needs of others.

## Psychotherapy

Visualisation has long been used to uncover and explore unconscious processes within psychotherapy. It is a feature of many important therapeutic approaches including psychoanalysis, Jungian analysis, Gestalt therapy, psychosynthesis, behaviour therapy, aversion therapy, arts and drama therapies, and oneirotherapy (for more information about these see two of my other books, *Time, Energy and the Psychology of Healing* and *Mental Imagery in Health Care*). Visualisation is used to enhance feelings of control and coping skills in various situations; to promote awareness of usually avoided situations and reduce fear of them; and to rehearse alternative strategies for dealing with situations. It is also a source of detail about past experiences and can provide access to significant memories of early childhood before language became predominant. It can promote a richer experience of a range of emotions, by-pass defences and resistances, and open up new avenues for exploration when therapy reaches an impasse.

Therapists generally prefer to work with a person's spontaneously produced visual images. However where a person's existing way of thinking is too limited to enable coping in a given area or where a therapist wishes to challenge a person's thinking, visualisation is often 'guided'. Guided imagery can be likened to a waking dream in which the subject, guided by another, imagines a new experience that enables the subject to confront the contents of his or her personal unconscious and relate these directly, and often dramatically, to life circumstances and problems. The effectiveness of guided visualisation has led to its widespread use within psychotherapy and counselling.

## Pain management

Visualisation is widely used in the health-care and related professions where its benefits are increasingly being recognised and supported by research. Physical pain is a difficult subject to talk about, especially for young children, and pain assessment based on visual imagery has been developed as a way of overcoming the limitations of language and providing reliable insight into children's suffering. Visualisation has also been used extensively to gain insight into factors such as guilt and anxiety that contribute to pain experience, and also to relieve pain. Visualisation now forms the basis of many modern pain management procedures promoted in pain clinics.

## Complementary medicine

It is quite probable that imaginative methods would have remained within the confines of psychotherapy had it not been for Carl Simonton, an American cancer specialist, and his wife Stephanie, a psychotherapist. Combining the insights derived from many different fields of research they argued that as emotional and mental factors, including stress, play a significant role both in susceptibility to and recovery from all disease, including cancer, the first step in getting well is to understand how these factors have contributed to illness and to find ways of influencing them in support of treatment. They also recognised that a cancer diagnosis in itself creates stress and other negative psychological responses such as fear, hopelessness and despair which further depress the immune system of the cancer patient, leading in many cases to a poor prognosis.

They believed that visualisation might help such patients in a number of ways: first by enabling the person to relax, so decreasing tension and counteracting the effects of stress. This, they suggested, would improve immune function. They considered that visualisation might also help cancer patients confront their fears of hopelessness and helplessness, enabling them to gain a sense of control and change in attitude. The visual images produced might also provide a means of accessing and exploring unhealthy beliefs hidden in the patient's unconscious mind and so yield valuable insights into their condition.

Carl Simonton taught his patients a simple form of relaxation and encouraged them to hold in their mind the image of a pleasant place. They were then asked to visualise their illness in any way it appeared to them, and the form of the treatment they were receiving. Having done this they were to imagine the cancer shrinking or otherwise responding in a positive way to treatment. Patients were also encouraged to imagine pain in the same way rather than trying to suppress it.

Of 159 patients with a diagnosis of a medically incurable malignancy treated over a 4 year period prior to 1978, none of whom were expected to live more than a year, 22.2 per cent were reported to have made a full recovery. The disease regressed in a further 17 per cent of patients and stabilised in 27 per cent. Further tumour growth was reported in 31 per cent of patients but average survival time increased by a factor of 1.5–2. Those who eventually succumbed to malignancy were reported as having maintained higher than usual levels of activity, and achieved a significant improvement in their quality of life.

Abundant anecdotal evidence, including accounts by children, has since supported the Simontons' claim that visualisation has an important role to play in the treatment of cancer as an adjunct to orthodox medical treatment. Subsequent studies have confirmed that visualisation has a number of effects, including cancer regression. It has been found to provide cancer patients with considerable relief from pain, nausea and anxiety and to be effective in reducing the aversiveness of cancer chemotherapy.

Although there is still need for carefully controlled studies, imaginative methods involving visualisation have been widely and enthusiastically adopted in the US and Europe. They have been promoted more cautiously in Britain but visualisation has been included in a number of orthodox hospital cancer treatment programmes. As yet there is no evidence to support claims for the effectiveness of visualisation in treating cancer in the absence of orthodox medical treatments such as surgery, chemotherapy and radiography.

## *Orthodox medicine*

Visualisation techniques have been shown to be effective in the treatment of a range of medical conditions including chronic pain, severe orthopaedic trauma, rheumatoid arthritis, diabetes, burn injury, alcoholism, stress disorders and childbirth. Improved immune function in response to visualisation has also been demonstrated, and its benefit in the treatment and management of AIDS has been recognised.

Visualisation is now also widely applied as an adjunct to orthodox medical approaches in diagnosis and treatment, and to relieve the pain and anxiety associated with many medical conditions. It is also used to help individuals and their families to cope with a wide range of illnesses and medical treatments, including radiotherapy, chemotherapy and surgery; and related issues such as death, bereavement, social isolation, trauma and disability.

## Self-healing and self-help

The claims made for visualisation are impressive and research supports its potency in a wide range of applications. However the claims are sometimes exaggerated. Some reports concerning its beneficial effects as an aid in the treatment of cancers and other serious illnesses have led to claims that imagery is a cure for cancer. Some individuals have advocated rejection of conventional medical treatment for cancer and AIDS in favour of visualisation techniques and lifestyle changes. There are undoubtedly those who attribute their personal cure to these factors, and they have been very influential in promoting visualisation as a method of self-help and healing, and its inclusion in treatment programmes for cancer and AIDS.

However, although there have been a great many anecdotal claims for the effects of visual imagery on diseases there is little convincing scientific evidence that *alone* it can cure serious illness. Nevertheless visual imagery from a wide variety of sources has been incorporated into self-healing approaches, and visualisation directed towards personal growth, psychological and spiritual transformation and positive mental health is widely pursued as a powerful and effective means of self-awareness and self-help. Visualisation is fundamental to the transformation of consciousness and the social and spiritual transition known as the New Age.

Ironically, although the wide and growing range of applications for visualisation in the clinical field appears highly innovative there is in fact nothing new about its use within medicine. In all the traditional systems of healing throughout the world since the earliest times healers have both diagnosed and treated illness by way of the visual images they evoked in their patients. The ancient Egyptians and Greeks used dream sanctuaries to elicit visual images that could provide clues to anxieties, fears, guilt and other emotional factors underpinning illness. They also used visual images to encourage positive expectations in their patients that could lead to cure.

Throughout history medical practitioners have quite deliberately exploited the power of the imagination in their use of placebos – imitation medicines or procedures with no intrinsic therapeutic value that are applied more to please and placate the person than for any organic purpose. Placebos have been demonstrated to be as or more effective than real medicine in the treatment of pain and a wide variety of diseases from hay fever to rheumatoid arthritis.

Attention has also focused on the negative placebo or nocebo effect whereby treatments known to be effective do not work because individuals do not expect them to. It appears that the success of any treatment depends to a large extent on whether or not the patient imagines that it can and will be effective, and so on the extent to which they can visualise or 'see' themselves getting better. From such a perspective all healing outcomes are self-generated and can be considered under the banner of 'self-healing' and 'self-help'. Greater understanding of the processes and potentialities of visualisation may lead in future to its more systematic application within medicine.

In the field of medicine no less than areas of business, commerce, education, science, sport and the arts, 'to accomplish great things we must not only act, but also dream' (Anatole France).

# 2

## BEGINNING VISUALISATION

Visualisation is not a specialised intellectual ability confined to highly creative individuals. It is an everyday ability we all engage in. Most of us have little or no difficulty creating visual images. Nevertheless, you may need practice before producing vivid visual images if you have neglected your imaginative abilities.

### Exercising Your Imagination

If you think of yourself as unimaginative or less imaginative than others this is almost certainly because you have not exercised your imagination, or have done so less than other people. The imagination needs exercise in order to function effectively. If it is not exercised regularly it will remain weak and undeveloped. Images will not be produced easily or spontaneously and will be vague, fleeting and difficult to sustain.

You may find the concept of 'exercising your imagination' off-putting. You may think that visualisation sounds like hard work and feel anxious that you might not be able to 'do' it correctly. However training the imagination is not like exercising the body. It does not require physical exertion. Nor does it require mental effort. In fact visualisation is not a matter of 'doing' anything. It is more a matter of 'being' open and receptive to aspects of yourself which emerge when the pressure to 'do' is relaxed. Being relaxed is the key to successful visualisation.

It is often claimed that you need to be deeply relaxed in order to produce imagery, and progressive relaxation techniques are invariably recommended prior to visualisation. Ordinarily, however, deep relaxation is not a necessary prerequisite for visualisation although it may be helpful if you are very tense, anxious or mentally overactive as these states can inhibit visualisation completely.

## Performance Anxiety

If you feel anxious that you might not be able to visualise this may reflect a general anxiety that performance, achievement, success, failure or evaluation, and the way these concerns create tensions in your life and limit your experience. Anxiety produces muscular tension and prevents relaxation and the production of visual images. Initial anxiety that you will not be able to 'do' visualisation increases the likelihood of this outcome.

You may find that your mind remains 'blank' when you begin visualisation. This is most likely to occur if you try too hard. 'Trying' is counterproductive because it involves effort and creates tensions which inhibit visualisation. You need to abandon it and 'allow' visual images to emerge spontaneously. You also need to allow sufficient time for this to occur.

## Regular Practice

Visualisation doesn't involve effort but it does require discipline. The more regularly you practise visualisation the easier it becomes and the more likely you are to achieve results. You are unlikely to 'find' time for visualisation and so you will have to 'make' or 'take' time for it. The time you allocate to visualisation will be determined by the purpose for which you wish to use it and how easily you can incorporate it into your daily routine. If you are using visualisation as an aid to relaxation, self-awareness, personal or spiritual development, problem solving or creative thinking, 20 to 30 minutes each day is normally enough. If you are using it in the treatment of illness, pain management, planning, learning, rehearsal, skilled performance or decision making several periods each day may be more appropriate. However 20 minutes is enough for each exercise period.

If you find it difficult to set aside 20 minutes daily for visualisation you might find it useful to consider the reasons for this and what it might indicate about you and your lifestyle.

If your mind becomes 'blank' when you begin visualisation it may be that you have not allowed sufficient time for images to emerge, and give up too soon. You may become impatient if images don't appear immediately. This produces tension rather than the relaxed state in which imagery is most easily produced and makes visualisation more difficult. If you find yourself becoming impatient with visualisation it may be that impatience also contributes to other difficulties you encounter in life.

# Preparing For Visualisation

The best time for visualisation is when it most suits you. Preferably this should not be just before retiring at night or when lying in bed, unless you are using visualisation to remedy insomnia, as you are likely to fall asleep. It may also be difficult to avoid sleep if you are too comfortable, but if you are uncomfortable you are unlikely to continue visualisation. For this reason it is advisable to practise visualisation when sitting comfortably in a position where your back, trunk and legs are well supported, with both feet set apart and firmly on the ground, your arms resting on your thighs or the arms of a chair, and no parts of the body twisted or crossed. You may wish to loosen restrictive clothing, remove your shoes and spectacles.

Closing your eyes may help you to visualise but it isn't essential. Most people produce visual imagery just as easily with their eyes open. The advantage of closing your eyes is that it reduces competing visual stimulation and allows you to pay closer attention to your imagery. However, if you wear contact lenses closing your eyes for any length of time will produce discomfort, so you may prefer to focus your eyes on a fixed point such as a mark on the floor or wall throughout visualisation. This will reduce competing visual stimulation. You should also follow this procedure if you are unable to close your eyes because of physical defects, surgery or injury.

Whatever time and/or place you choose for visualisation, try, initially at least, to keep to these every day. With practice external stimuli can easily be screened out and so the setting in which you undertake visualisation is largely irrelevant. I have successfully led visualisation classes in a busy hospital ward, above a dance studio, in noisy classrooms and in competition with fire alarms, ambulance sirens, loud traffic, thunderstorms and gales. Feeling at ease is more important than context. Most people are initially more troubled by the presence of strangers or too many friends/acquaintances than the setting when they begin visualisation. It is therefore important that you find somewhere you can feel safe and fairly relaxed.

In practice this often proves difficult. Many people who begin visualisation do not continue even when they gain benefits from it. This is particularly true of women who feel 'guilty' about taking time for themselves or who worry that others might consider them self-indulgent if they do so. Many men also feel guilty about 'taking it easy' when they have work to 'do', a living to earn and other goals to achieve. If you are anxious about what your family, friends or window cleaner might think of you were they to discover you with your eyes closed 'doing nothing', find somewhere away from others where you will be undisturbed, even if this means locking the bathroom door and soaking in the bath for 20 minutes.

If you find it difficult to discipline yourself to practise visualisation regularly you may prefer to join an exercise class or group, or to form your own, working through and discussing afterwards with a partner or friend(s) a series of exercises such as those presented later in this book. This can be very valuable and enjoyable. Nevertheless you need to practise visualisation regularly in order to produce results.

# Initial Difficulties

## *Mind wandering*

You may be less worried by an inability to produce visual images than the prospect of your imagination running wild. Rather than give it a free rein you may try to control it by keeping a grip on yourself. A jockey controls a race-horse in much the same way, tightening the grip on the reins and turning the horse around so that it moves in circles and cannot progress forward. If you don't give yourself 'your head' when you begin visualisation you will find that your mind wanders around in much the same way, turning again and again to certain issues and not progressing beyond them.

## Censoring and directing images

If you find your imagination playing tricks – producing imagery that is unexpected or unacceptable – you may attempt to censor or direct it. This defeats the whole point of the exercise just as surely as 'pulling up' a horse prevents it running free. When beginning visualisation you should be aware of the image that first comes to mind and allow sufficient time for it to develop and become clear. Do not resist other images forming or seize them impatiently as they emerge and fail to allow any of them to develop fully.

## Losing control

If you are to allow your imagination to run free you must allow the 'jockey' – your rational mind – to relax and let go of the thoughts, anxieties, concerns and preoccupations that dominate your ordinary everyday thinking. However, fear of losing control – of losing your mind – even temporarily, may be a source of anxiety. You may also feel anxious if you believe that by relaxing your conscious mind you may become unconscious. If anything consciousness or aware-ness is enhanced during visualisation, and self-control increases. Letting go of the constraints normally imposed by rational conscious thoughts enables you not only to become aware of the physical, physiological, emotional and psychological processes ordinarily beyond your conscious control but also to influence them directly. This is precisely how visualisation achieves its effects.

## Becoming irrational

You may be anxious about becoming 'lost' in fantasy; that you may lose yourself or your mind by looking inwards. In our culture introversion or looking inwards is often seen as producing withdrawn and other-worldly people who gradually lose touch with reality. It therefore tends to be seen as undesirable.

You might find it more useful to think of visualisation as a way of removing yourself temporarily from unpleasant realities of the physical world into a more affable world of fantasy. If for this reason only, visualisation is of considerable benefit, and is a problem only when it becomes a permanent retreat from reality. As one psychologist has observed, it is one thing to build a castle in the sky but quite another to try and live in it.

## Being detached

By contrast, you may be anxious because you think that you are insufficiently immersed in your fantasy. You may imagine yourself in scenes in a detached manner as though looking down on yourself and worry that you are visualising incorrectly. This in no way reduces the validity or potency of the imagery and is quite usual initially. You can use imagery very effectively without ever becoming fully immersed in it.

## Being childish

You may be concerned that visualisation is childish or silly and be unwilling to engage in it or admit to doing so for this reason. There is little doubt that visualisation is a childish activity. For children fantasy is reality. The inner world of pictures, which as adults they often have to rediscover, is already there. It is natural rather than created by any technique and is the source of their creativity and learning. Encouraging their imagination and its expression improves their ability to cope and learn. It is therefore not silly. What *is* silly is that so many adults limit their coping strategies and capacity for creative living by neglecting their imagination.

## Encountering hidden dangers

You may fear that by looking inwards into the hidden or 'occult' aspects of yourself you will encounter evil and terrible features and lose your soul rather than your mind. Such fears are often encouraged by ministers of religion and others who view this ordinarily hidden domain as the realm of the devil.

It is because their hidden, darker or shadowy features are often considered crazy, evil or sinful that people may wish not simply to hide but to rid themselves of them. However, a number of good qualities such as normal instincts, appropriate reactions, realistic insights and creative impulses may also be hidden. If these are resisted or denied physical and psychological illness can occur. In order to be fully integrated, whole or healthy you need to confront these features. They must be brought into consciousness and recognised. This process is healthy and beneficial.

However, experiencing images that emerge from and reveal aspects of this ordinarily invisible realm may be emotionally painful, unpalatable or unpleasant, and you may strongly resist them. If you examine this resistance it invariably reveals negative beliefs and expectancies about yourself which prevent you achieving successful outcomes. These negative attitudes can only be changed if they are brought to the surface.

## Identifying Resistance

Preoccupations with aches, pains, minor irritations, noises, draughts and the like are typical ways in which we avoid engaging in imagery. Such avoidance invariably conceals our resistance to looking into ourselves. Identifying these tendencies may help you to become aware of the resistance you need to overcome if you are to use visualisation effectively.

You may not want to look too closely at the hidden or unknown aspects of yourself, either out of fear of what you will find or because of the implications it might have for your life. Consequently you will hold on to your problems rather than take responsibility for change. If you can identify with these concerns it is important that you try to confront the consequences of the change you fear.

You may not be aware that you are reluctant to look at yourself, and so deny that you are. However, this tendency may be revealed in your reactions to visualisation. You may 'get nowhere' with it because you 'drift off' or fall asleep. Sleep is often a way of evading tasks we don't wish to perform. It is a way of avoiding ourselves, our responsibilities and fears. However, as John le Carré (*The Russia House*, p. 122) observes, 'By changing nothing we hang on to what we understand, even if it is the bars of our own gaol'. Confronting yourself is liberating, so closer examination of the images that evoke a 'cagey' reaction within you is desirable.

Visualisation may challenge your beliefs or compromise your view of yourself in significant ways. You may believe that it is wrong for you to take time for visualisation. 'Shoulds' and 'should nots' like these often generate stress, illness and dysfunctional (disturbed or abnormal) behaviour. Even if you give yourself permission to take some time for yourself and relax, these self-imposed imperatives may prevent you from doing so effectively. Jean, for example, enjoyed imagining herself sitting in a fragrant pine forest until an imaginary smell like burning toast reminded her that she should not be neglecting her domestic chores. This prevented her continuing visualisation. If you can identify with Jean you may benefit from examining the rules of conduct you impose on yourself and the anxiety and problems they generate.

If you are unable to produce images this may indicate that you are resisting self-awareness. If you encounter this difficulty it is important not merely to accept it but also to examine what is stopping you doing so. You may find that although ordinarily you have little or no difficulty with visualisation you find certain images problematic. It may be that this particular image challenges your view of yourself or beliefs that you hold. You may, for example, resist certain images because they seem 'unmanly' or 'unfeminine', or challenge your views on other issues. This probably reflects lack of self-confidence because any views or beliefs that won't stand up to challenge are not strong.

If you find that you are resisting or 'blocking' certain images try to identify the excuses and explanations you are inclined to offer. You might, for example, believe that you are unable to respond or 'get into' an image of yourself jumping into the sea because you are frightened of water, or can't swim. Irrespective of any symbolic significance that water might have for you, such a response highlights the way in which your conscious preconceived views restrict your experience even at the fantasy level, and the extent to which certain expectations and beliefs (usually negative) impose limitations by preventing you exploring different responses or creating new experiences for yourself.

This difficulty may be more marked if you are using creative visualisation to achieve specific outcomes. In their work with cancer sufferers Carl and Stephanie Simonton found that some patients are unable or unwilling to engage in visualisation because they believe that to imagine their cancer shrinking when they had been told it is growing constitutes lying. Visualisation therefore compromises their views of reality, and possibly also their view of themselves as honest. It is important to realise that creative visualisation is not a method of self-deception but a means of self-direction and that what is being imagined is the desired outcome rather than what is happening at the time. The belief that you are deluding yourself by imagining your body eliminating a cancer may conceal a strong fear of the disease and doubt about the body's ability to overcome it. Therefore you should closely examine images you have difficulty creating, accepting or wish to change, and the reasons for this.

You may resist imagery because you don't want to get well or solve your problems. Once again it is desirable to consider the reasons for this. You may not be fully conscious of them, in which case wherever you encounter resistance to visualisation it is worth asking yourself what you stand to gain if you improve your present condition and circumstances, and what you might lose.

It may be that you don't want to look at certain aspects of your life because the time is not appropriate. If this is the case then by all means 'give up' visualisation until such time when you welcome rather than resist the insights it provides and are willing to change.

## Acknowledging Imagery

Initially you may be uncertain whether what you 'see in your mind's eye' is imaginary. You may think that unless images are wholly invented they are not truly imaginary. You may dismiss images as merely your memory. If so this suggests that you may confuse objective and subjective realities – that is, you may have difficulty distinguishing between the world 'out there' and your inner world.

You may believe that because an object or scene you visualise has or had a counterpart in the objective world your imagery is objective and 'real' rather than a subjective inner representation of these features of the outer world. If so, you may dismiss the potential significance of images you produce because it has a physical counterpart in your present or past. If you find yourself querying the validity of your imagery in this way ask yourself why, of all the objects, people or scenes that you might have imagined, you 'brought to mind' this particular one. As your creation it expresses something of you, the creator. What might that be? Examine the image closely to see what you can discover and learn from it.

Much of what you take to be 'real' in the world is imaginary. If you regard reality as an immutable, objective domain outside of yourself, in some way fixed and beyond your control you may not realise the extent to which you create that reality through your beliefs, assumptions, expectations and imaginings, and thus the degree of choice you have in determining your life. If the events and circumstances of your life appear fixed and your responses to them seem unavoidable, you are likely to perceive some degree of stress as inevitable. If this is so, you may find it difficult to accept that you can create a different reality by cultivating a different outlook or attitude, seeing things in a different light or envisioning other possibilities, and may as a result be able to solve problems and reduce or eliminate stress.

If you have difficulty accepting that your images are not 'real', you may not realise that other 'realities' of your existence such as fears, anxieties, expectations and assumptions, self and body images and identity may also be wholly or partly imaginary, and a source of unnecessary and avoidable problems. For many people 'reality', comprising as it does fantasy ideas about the self, others and the world, imaginary threats and fears, is largely imaginary. Problems arise because we are 'hooked' on this fantasy and cannot distinguish it from reality. Much aggression, for example, is a response to imagined insults, and fear may arise through anticipated rather than actual danger.

Visualisation enables you to confront and accept the reality of who and what you are rather than fantasy ideals. Exposing and exploring rather than ignoring your imagery can prevent you becoming bound up in fantasy. You can use it to contact qualities within yourself, to express your personal power and potentials and act in the outside world. You can move from being frightened by your dreams, dominated by fantasies and anxieties that cut you off from the real world, to having more of your personal power available to live your life creatively in the present.

## Recording Your Images

Repeating imagery exercises like those provided in this book is desirable because the insights they provide will alter as you and your life situation change. You might assume that you will produce the same images in response to these exercises however many times you repeat them. You will find that this is rarely the case. Where it is, it is probably because you are resisting new insights and change. When you reproduce similar imagery novel and/or additional insights usually emerge also. For this reason, and because images are only fleeting and quickly forgotten, however intense or significant they may be, you should record them.

The record may be in the form of an audio-recording or written log book. Audio-recording is quick and immediate. It enables you to detail your experiences as they are occurring and provides a 'sound-track' which not only highlights various features but also enables them to be reviewed subsequently. However it is not always convenient and it restricts the record to verbal content, when the purpose of visualisation is to encourage integration of verbal and non-verbal thinking.

A written record has most of the drawbacks of audio-recording and lacks immediacy. It is also rather laborious. The complexity of many images and their simultaneous presentation often makes any verbal account daunting and inadequate. So a verbal and visual record of experiences, in words and pictures, which includes sketches and paintings, may be more appropriate. What might be thought of as a 'pictionary' can also be a helpful appendix to this record. This is a separate record of your interpretations of specific images that enables you to build up your own symbolic vocabulary.

The images you produce and record do not need to make 'sense'. There may be no conscious, verbal connections between your images and the subjects they represent. It is sufficient simply to know who or what is represented by a particular symbol so that when you encounter it again you recognise it as relating to your feelings about that subject.

Certain features of your imagery will tend to recur in different contexts and detail over time so that initially what may appear obscure, meaningless or trivial becomes progressively more clear, intelligible, relevant and significant. Your record should therefore include details of incidental and coincidental experiences and insights which occur as a result of visualisation rather than during it, such as when a feature or theme arising in an exercise recurs or is amplified in a subsequent dream, reverie or actual life experience. 'Coincidences' such as these are invariably highly significant but are often overlooked or dismissed. You may later find in a book, magazine or newspaper an exact or almost exact representation of your images. Including illustrative material such as this in your record is helpful because it will not only jog your memory but also help to clarify your thoughts about images and their meaning.

Practising visualisation may produce 'side-effects' inasmuch that it tends to stimulate a good deal of thought and other unconscious processes such as dreaming. It is therefore not unusual to encounter the same motifs or symbols in subsequent dreams, day-dreams or fantasies. Dreams may give you insight into previously unfathomed images, and visualisation may clarify the content of your dreams.

It seems that once the 'bridge' between the conscious and unconscious aspects of yourself has been opened, the unconscious will take every opportunity to use it. Dreaming typically becomes more frequent and more vivid. If you have not previously dreamed in colour you may begin to do so. It may also impress itself more powerfully than it did, so you might find that you may begin to remember your dreams where previously you have not; or you may remember more of them.

Keeping a record helps you to cultivate a disciplined approach to self-examination. A record of this kind is particularly important if images are being used in the treatment of illness, in rehabilitation, or to improve sporting, musical or other skilled performance, where certain kinds of outcome are desired. In such cases, it is advisable to establish that the images you are using are suitable to the task in hand.

It is particularly important to keep a record over time because the effects of visualisation tend to be progressive and cumulative. Your record need not be a literary masterpiece or a work of art. It is essentially an *aide-mémoire*, enabling you to refer back to earlier images, and to keep a track of both process and progress. With time you will find that you are able to focus and concentrate on your images more fully and will perceive greater detail in them than formerly. Its most important function, however, is in helping you to understand what is happening now.

## Identifying With Imagery

It is helpful to record imagery verbally in the first person, present tense. The personalisation of imagery in this way not only locates the experience in the immediate present but also helps to prevent projection, where you attribute responsibility for your personal creations or products (whether imaginings, thoughts, feelings, pains, actions or illnesses) to external causes. The projection of personal features on to the outside world and others makes us think that these external forces are responsible for, or cause them. Typically we use phrases such as 'It makes me sick' or 'angry' rather than 'I make myself sick or angry' in response to who or whatever it might be. Even more impersonal is the use of the word 'one'. In both cases a verbal ploy distances us from ourselves as the source of our feelings and responsibility for them, implying that their source is external and beyond our control. The personalisation of images by using the first person, present tense works in reverse. It helps you to acknowledge personal responsibility and your sense of being effective in the world rather than a passive victim of circumstance; and awareness of your contribution to problems and illnesses.

This verbal shift also helps you to identify your imagery as a specific personal creation for which you are responsible, and which, for this very reason, is almost certainly meaningful when you examine it closely. If you cannot easily see the relevance of an image when you view it objectively you may feel quite differently if you personalise it. So, for example, 'I imagine a cool, unmoving pool with murky depths' becomes 'I am a cool, unmoving pool with murky depths' which, at the very least, gives food for thought.

## Interpreting Imagery

One of the most widespread misconceptions about working with images is that they have universal meanings known to 'experts' who can interpret them. This mistaken view owes much to the 'authoritative' interpretations of dream and fantasy imagery by psychologists. It is perpetrated in books on dreams and other imagery. In fact, while your imagery may have certain universal features it represents none the less your own unique symbolic language or representational system which you must learn to translate and understand. Two individuals may produce the same imagery but it may have quite different meanings for them.

Christine was puzzled by the gilt fish she visualised frequently. This made no sense to her until it was suggested that this image might relate to guilt. This triggered an immediate response. In her determination to provide her daughter with a healthy diet Christine insisted she ate fish regularly, until she discovered that the child was allergic to fish and that this was the cause of her chronic health problems. Christine still felt guilty about this even though the problem had been identified and remedied some years before.

When Phyllis first began visualisation she found that a fish would also appear in every situation she imagined. She couldn't make sense of this as it seemed totally unrelated to the other features of the imagery. When asked by other members of her group to describe it more fully she realised it wasn't a real fish but was made of glass. This made even less sense to her, but when questioned as to what she associated with it she immediately recognised it as an ornament given to her as a present by her mother. Although she disliked it intensely she had dutifully displayed the fish on the mantelpiece when her mother visited but otherwise hid it. When her mother died it was consigned to the loft and some years later was given away. However, once relieved of the fish Phyllis began to feel very guilty not only because it highlighted many differences between her and her mother as to what was 'tasteful', desirable and acceptable, but also because she had disliked and rejected her mother's genuine and well-meant gift to her. She realised that the fish symbolised her feelings towards her mother, and when she re-examined her visualisations in this light they provided profoundly meaningful insights into her relationship with her mother and its implications for her life.

Interpretation of your imagery by others, however 'expert', will reveal details of their symbolism rather than yours and may be highly misleading. So like Christine and Phyllis, you must explore your own symbolic vocabulary, its meanings and usage.

You can do this by carefully examining the context of your images and other available clues, their components, similar kinds of images, the associations they evoke, the memories they stir and the responses they produce. In this way you will become expert in your own symbols. If you work with others in this enterprise you should ensure that the personal meaning of your symbols is not lost in its translation by them, and that you do not impose your personal meanings on their imagery.

## Understanding Your Imagery

You may realise only too clearly that your images are significant, without knowing what their meaning is. Most of us tend to look outside ourselves for answers and solutions rather than within. This reflects not only our tendency to project responsibility on to others but also the outward looking tendency of Western culture, which encourages respect for authorities and experts, especially in the health field. However, the major challenge of self-help, especially as regards health, is for us to assume the responsibility to become the ultimate authority on ourselves, and to acknowledge this.

Nevertheless, the meaning of your imagery will not always be immediately obvious and you may need help to understand it. Without help you may be left puzzled, confused, alarmed and, in some instances, distressed by images and the powerful feelings that sometimes accompany them. If 'untranslated' images are rehearsed without comprehension of their full meaning the resulting outcome may be far from what is intended or desired, especially if the images are inappropriate, self-defeating or futile. For example, a woman who repeatedly visualised her body's healing forces 'destroying' the virulent weed that represented her illness only realised after some considerable time that the foam was not the powerful herbicide she had first thought but harmless soap. Similarly, limiting and negative thoughts can reduce the likelihood of positive outcomes and effects from visualisation. For example, the healing force 'mobilised' by one man in an attempt to prevent the spread of a rapidly advancing cancer consisted of two men blocking off a flooded underground railway tunnel with a portable cement-mixer, a bucket and two spades. Inappropriate imagery such as this is unlikely to be effective.

## Brain-storming

Working with imagery is like puzzling over a vast jigsaw and trying to establish the connections between its many features. This is achieved primarily by identifying the links between elements. Simple word association may be effective, but you should avoid the tendency to generate lists of words. It is preferable to 'brain-storm' by writing or drawing the image or its component features in the centre of a large piece of paper or blackboard. You can then add to this all the words and pictures you associate with it. Each associated item can be 'mapped' on to the paper, by placing each one, as it emerges, close to the word or picture that triggered it, until no further associations can be made or the available space is used up. You can include drawings, paintings, various kinds of artwork and colour. In this way you can produce thousands of items, each linked to the others. You can make connections between items by joining them. This results in a huge circular plan like a mandala or web which represents a mental map far more rich and varied than the linear pattern of associations lists typically produce.

These mandalas can be used not only to help you to amplify and elaborate images but also to generate ideas, plan essays and projects, and stimulate creative thinking of all kinds. Nevertheless as most of us have been educated and trained to organise our thoughts in lists and flow diagrams you will probably find that you need a good deal of practice before you feel comfortable with this procedure, and can use it effectively.

Images often generate both verbal and visual puns and you should include these in your map. Puns and ambiguities are often highly significant, as Christine's perplexing 'gilt fish' (p. 44) shows, and you should examine them carefully.

## Other ways of working on imagery

You can work on imagery in many other ways. A striking illustration of one of these is presented in Steven Spielberg's film *Close Encounters of the Third Kind*. Its hero attempts to clarify a vague mental impression he has formed of a landscape by drawing, modelling in clay and mashed potato, earthworking and various other constructions. In this way he refines the image sufficiently to be able to recognise its 'real-life' counterpart when this is shown briefly on television. This also shows the way in which coincidence often serves to amplify, illuminate and resolve puzzling imagery.

Imaginary scenes may be dramatised using cartoon figures, puppets, dolls, toys, other persons, or by acting out or talking through each of the 'parts' of the fantasy in turn. You can role-play the themes or characters of imagery, and even develop board games for this purpose.

You can use many of these methods when working alone or with others, guided by books and other media, or when guided directly by others on a one-to-one or group basis. In this way you may begin to recognise and understand elements of your personal symbolism, and the meanings of themes in which certain symbols recur.

## Seeking help

You may find that the meaning of certain images becomes clear as a result of other activities, in sudden flashbacks or images, or flashes of insight, which in some cases may be dramatic. Whereas this latter 'Eureka' effect usually brings about a sudden transformation of consciousness, understanding or awareness, images may recur without any increased insight or understanding. You should not dismiss or ignore these but carefully note them. Usually resolution will occur quite spontaneously, but as with medical symptoms that persist despite treatment, it is advisable to seek assistance if troubling images persist for an appreciable time.

Other people, whether therapists, writers or friends,

can have a valuable role in helping you to understand your imagery. They can help you to explore your feelings and responses to images and the associations they have for you. They can also amplify your responses to imagery by expressing the associations and responses your images elicit in them; by pointing to similar symbols in mythology and esoteric traditions, and by suggesting possible meanings. Nevertheless you should not encourage or allow them to 'interpret' your images for you.

It may well be that without the guidance and assistance of others you will find it difficult to make much sense of your imagery and discontinue visualisation. Competing demands, pressures and activities, lack of support and affirmation from family and friends rather than lack of interest, enthusiasm or discipline are most likely to prevent you taking time to familiarise yourself with visualisation or to put time aside for it. These factors will undermine effective outcomes, and should be borne in mind when you begin visualisation.

# 3

# HELPING YOURSELF TO RELAX

Visualisation aids relaxation, and you may be attracted to it for this reason. Relaxation is a letting go of and freedom from habitual physical and psychological tension. It is the opposite of nervous hypertension (a state of high tension) which has long been recognised as a feature of many physical and psychological conditions, and behavioural problems. Relaxation or rest is therefore viewed as the antidote to all ills and is widely recommended in their treatment.

## Are You Relaxed?

Advising people to relax is usually quite futile because they don't know how to, so 'rest cures' rarely live up to the name. Relaxation is not achieved simply by lying in bed, lounging in front of the television or having a few drinks with friends. It is an integrated shift in physiological functions that is rarely, if ever, achieved without training and practice. You may appear relaxed when lying quietly on a sofa, but no significant physiological change may occur, even after several hours. Even when you feel relaxed mental activity, physical excitement and muscular tension may remain, and be revealed in irregular breathing, elevated pulse rate, involuntary or local reflexes such as wrinkling of the forehead, tightness of the facial muscles and swallowing. By contrast, when you are truly relaxed all tension is absent, breathing loses its irregularity, pulse rate drops, limbs lack firmness and are soft and limp, and there is no reflex swallowing or blinking.

Normally people cannot judge accurately whether or not they are relaxed. They are unaware that their muscles are tense, even when tension is extreme. What they consider to be relaxation or rest is in many instances inadequate. Attempts to relax or rest may prove counterproductive as restlessness may give rise to distress and vice versa.

## Inducing Relaxation

Traditionally relaxation procedures have been based on the premise that you can only begin to relax when you know what tension is and how you produce it, and that by realising how to tighten a muscle you can just as easily learn how to 'undo' it. This involves learning to identify tension in the muscle groups of your body by tightening them and then ceasing to do so. Most methods of relaxation aim to produce progressively an extreme degree of neuro-muscular relaxation and to train the body to react in the desired manner as and when required. Even so, tension disappears only gradually and relaxation is slow and progressive rather than sudden and immediate. The process is initially rather lengthy and requires regular practice.

However, although relaxation can be thought of as the cultivation of muscle sense or bodily awareness it is much more than this. Complete relaxation is possible only when all mental processes are suspended. This is because bodily tensions are produced in response to mental attitudes, preoccupations and concerns, and the resulting emotional tensions, conflicts, fears and anxieties. If psychological tensions are not relaxed physical relaxation is difficult, and at best, limited.

For example, Bob was able to relax so effectively that he could no longer feel his body, but as soon as he stopped focusing on 'undoing' the tightness in his muscles he would begin to think about his financial difficulties and would immediately become tense again.

Psychological tensions are largely a function of rational, logical verbal thinking; a response to the endless stream of words in our heads that occupy most of our waking moments. This is ordinarily suspended during sleep, and then only gradually, allowing non-verbal thought to emerge in the images of dreams. Verbal thought spontaneously gives way to visual and other sensory imagery in certain other circumstances such as fantasy, reverie and day-dreaming. Verbal thought may also be suspended during any activity that absorbs us, whether this is fishing, crocheting, painting or dancing. For this reason we find such activities relaxing and pursue them when at leisure.

Relaxation can also be induced deliberately by various methods which aim to reduce or 'turn down the volume' of verbal thoughts. These methods, which include most forms of meditation, biofeedback, hypnosis, self-hypnosis and autogenic training, all involve visualisation to achieve this effect.

In order to discover how visualisation assists relaxation you might like to compare the following exercises. The first exercise is derived from standard progressive relaxation techniques, and does not include visualisation. The only difference with the second exercise is that it includes visualisation.

## EXERCISE 1

### Progressive Relaxation

Find somewhere you can sit comfortably and having done so simply be aware of how your body is located in relation to its surroundings. Be aware of your feelings in this situation. How *do* you feel? Do you feel silly, or guilty about taking time to do the exercise? Do you feel anxious or concerned that you might not be able to do it? Do you feel impatient to get on with it? Having identified how you feel, close your eyes or focus them upon a fixed point or object within your line of vision, such as a mark on a wall, ceiling or floor. Then gradually withdraw your attention from your surroundings and bring it to the boundary between your body and adjacent surfaces. As you do so notice whether the contact is comfortable or painful and adjust your position so as to maximise comfort and minimise pain.

When you are positioned as comfortably as possible bring your attention to your toes. Tighten them for a moment or so and then let go of the tightness, noticing its effect not simply on your toes and feet but the rest of your body. Repeat this once or twice and then bring your attention to your lower legs and do likewise. Having done so work your way upwards tightening and releasing each of the major parts of your body in turn; your thighs, buttocks, lower back, stomach, shoulders, arms and hands, neck, face and jaw. If any parts of your body remain tense, tight or painful spend a few minutes tightening and releasing them until you feel an overall reduction of tightness in your body.

Then focus on your breathing. Spend a few moments observing your breathing, noting whether it is deep or shallow, rapid or slow, even or erratic. Breathe more deeply and as you do so let go of any remaining tension in your body. Continue breathing in this way for a further 10 or 20 minutes, observing any thoughts, impressions, sensations that arise but without holding on to them. Then allow your awareness to return to normal.

## Commentary

You will probably find that this procedure is good for identifying muscle tension and pain. Jane thought she was fairly comfortable and relaxed until she focused on her muscles in this way and realised just how tense many of them were. It made her more aware of how tense she is normally and how she can deal with it. Trying this method for the first time Julie found that her tension was mainly located in her head. With practice she found that she could relax her entire body by relaxing the muscles of her head, and especially those of her jaw. Once she could do this the severe tension headaches she had suffered for many years were eliminated. However, pain or infirmity may prevent the muscular contractions required in most progressive relaxation procedures. Patricia, who still suffered painful after-effects of a whiplash injury to her neck, found the very prospect of tensing it created anxiety and prevented her relaxing.

## Drawbacks of progressive relaxation

A major drawback of relaxation procedures that focus on muscle tightening is that they can create greater tension and anxiety. Most people find it is easier to tighten their muscles than to release them with the result that when they increase the tension in their body they tend to retain it. Their overall level of tension is therefore increased rather than reduced. This increase in tension may be accompanied by anxiety, panic or other unpleasant feelings. Mike, for example, experienced a dramatic spiral of tension and anxiety when the existing tension in his stomach region was exaggerated, producing feelings of nausea. This in turn generated anxiety that he might vomit, and further tension as he tried to bring the anxiety and unpleasant physical sensations under control. If, like Mike, you began the exercise wondering whether you should or could do it, you may have found that the associated tension and anxiety intensified rather than decreased.

Another common difficulty with this kind of progressive relaxation procedure is that it tends to be tedious. You may have found yourself becoming impatient or bored, and more tense as a result.

The major limitation of this kind of approach is, however, that it maintains precisely the logical, rational, analytical thinking that characterises verbal thought, which is precisely what relaxation procedures aim to suspend.

You may find that other aspects of Exercise 1 create uncertainty and anxiety. It may be that uncertainty about *where* to focus attention on your breathing generated anxiety and increased tension. Most probably you focused attention on either your chest or navel. Your attention was probably diverted from your breathing by intrusive thoughts and you may have become anxious because of your inability to focus. Janet, for example, found that worrying about being unable to relax made her more tense. Like her, you may have worried not only that you were not 'doing' the exercise correctly but that you cannot do so because you are unable to suspend your thoughts. If you were able to focus on your breathing you may have become anxious as you became aware of sensations of pulsation, loudness or irregularity.

As a result of this increased tension you may be unable to relax using procedures that focus primarily on muscle tightening. Even if you can achieve relaxation in this way you may experience sudden anxiety or even panic. This is because the sensations associated with relaxation – wooziness, lightness, falling, floating, vibrations, tingling and loss of sensation in limbs – are strange if you have only rarely or never experienced them.

Even if you have not experienced any of the above difficulties you will probably find that Exercise 2, which includes imagery, enables you to relax more easily and fully. Try it, and compare the process and outcomes with those of the previous exercise.

## EXERCISE 2

### Relaxation with Visualisation

Find somewhere to sit comfortably and having done so become aware of how your body is located in relation to its surroundings. Then close your eyes or focus on a fixed point or object within your line of vision, such as a mark on a wall, ceiling or floor. Having done so, gradually draw your attention from your surroundings and bring it to the boundary between your body and adjacent surfaces. As you do so notice whether the contact is uncomfortable or painful, and adjust your position so as to maximise comfort and minimise pain.

When you are positioned as comfortably as possible bring your attention to your right arm, then down your arm into the hand. Imagine that you are holding in that hand an ancient gold coin. It is the only one of its kind known to exist and is therefore priceless. Grip your imaginary coin so tightly that there is no possibility of it slipping from your hand, and as you do so observe the effects of this action, not only in your hand, lower arm, upper arm and shoulder, but also in your neck, head, jaw and elsewhere in your body. Follow the effects of this action as far as they extend and until you can feel a tremor developing in your arm. When the action is becoming too painful or unpleasant to sustain further, carefully transfer the coin to your left hand, once again gripping it so tightly that there is no danger of it being lost. Follow the effect to its furthest extremity and tighten your grip until you can feel a tremor in your arm. When you can feel this toss the coin from the left hand to the right and then throw it away, allowing the fingers of both hands to drop loosely as you do so and your arms to fall by your sides.

Now imagine that the floor beneath you is beginning to rise. Resist this as forcefully as you can, spreading the fingers and the palms of your hands flat and pushing downwards. The floor continues to rise, forcing your hands upwards and obliging you to flex your arms against it. If the floor continues to rise you will be squashed against the ceiling, so press downwards with all your strength. Despite this the floor continues to rise, until, just as it seems you cannot resist further, the floor falls away and your arms and hands with it. Allow your arms to flop at your side and take a few seconds to experience this sensation and allow it to spread throughout your body.

When you have done so, bring your attention to your stomach. Observe your breathing there for a few moments. Now imagine that you are lying flat and there is a saucer and teacup positioned over your navel. Breathe in deeply, allowing your abdomen to fill with air and observe the saucer and cup as they rise. When the cup is as high as it can rise hold your breath for a second or so, keeping the cup still and then breathe out slowly, watching the cup sink downwards as you do so. Breathe in and out for a few moments watching the movements of the cup and saucer.

Having done so take your attention to your chest. Imagine that on your chest there is a butterfly which has just emerged from its cocoon and is drying its wings in the sun. Breathe in and out deeply and with each in-breath imagine that you are breathing life into the butterfly and that it is spreading its wings more and more. Continue to breathe in and out deeply until the butterfly seems about to fly off. At the point where it seems about to take flight breathe out and observe what happens. Then allow the image of the butterfly to fade and bring your attention to the tip of your nose. Observe the sensations there as you breathe in and out.

Having done so imagine that you are breathing in coloured light through your nose. This enters your body and is drawn down your spine to its base where it curls upward. As you breathe out it is drawn upwards, forcing a dark dense fog towards and out of your mouth, leaving your body feeling light and clear. Continue breathing in this way for a few moments, before allowing yourself to return to normal awareness.

## Commentary

You will probably find that you feel more relaxed following this exercise than after Exercise 1. Most people relax much more easily and quickly when relaxation procedures involve visualisation. When focusing on imagery they tend to forget about trying to relax and as a result they relax effortlessly. The images provide a focus for both mental and muscular activity and enable you to become more fully involved or absorbed. The experience is, as a result, more complete and this often produces significant reactions.

## Reactions to the exercise

You may have experienced a sudden release of emotion when you imagined letting go of the coin or the butterfly taking flight. Crying, feeling overwhelmingly sad or angry are all common reactions to these images. They occur because you respond as a unified whole to various influences rather than solely mentally or physically. When you experience pain or hurt you defend yourself against future trauma of this kind by contracting various muscles. If you maintain these contractions over time they come to characterise you. These defensive 'character structures' are reflected in your posture and in your entire behaviour, often setting up patterns of dysfunction and disease. As you begin to relax these muscles the feelings they are defending are released spontaneously, so as you let go physically you also experience a release of held-in emotions. You may also experience images related to the circumstances that initially provoked the defensive response; a person, place, situation or object might spontaneously 'come to mind'.

Holding on to the imaginary coin often produces images that provide insight into what you are holding on to in life or are trying to maintain a grip on. Similarly images may emerge as you resist the rising floor and these can provide insight into what you are resisting in life and the physical effects of this resistance.

Letting go of the coin or the butterfly is often accompanied by memories of loss and feelings of grief and sadness. Sometimes there are no accompanying images, only inexplicable feelings. If you habitually defend yourself against loss, albeit unconsciously, you may find it difficult to let go of the coin or the butterfly. Rather than release the butterfly you will try to prevent it flying. You may try to

**61**

keep it 'close to your chest' and harm or destroy it in the process.

## Focusing on breathing

You probably found that by focusing on your breathing at the navel it became deeper, slower and more steady. Like most people you may have realised that ordinarily your breathing is very shallow, and that by breathing more deeply you become more relaxed.

Focus on breathing at the chest also produces slower, deeper breathing and reactions to the butterfly often provide insight into some of the underlying tensions of your life. Paul imagined a small colourless butterfly without substance, and realised that this reflected his belief that he didn't 'amount to much' and his low self-esteem. Similarly, Mary's butterfly seemed weak and insignificant at close quarters but larger the further it flew away from her, reflecting her anxiety that others would be disappointed if they came close to her. Jane imagined watching her butterfly 'working hard to rise' and catch an air thermal that would carry it in the right direction, only to become worried that it was exposed and vulnerable. Upon reflection she realised that this represents the anxiety she feels about becoming successful.

By itself focus on breathing at the nose slows and deepens breathing and produces greater relaxation. Indeed this is the basis of a traditional meditation used in India for stilling the mind. Nevertheless it has a major drawback in that initially, at least, it may not be sufficiently absorbing to hold attention. Intrusive thoughts may therefore become more seductive and difficult to banish. Breathing in colour produces much greater absorption and for this reason is a feature of many traditional meditation procedures of the East and also contemporary Western practices such as colour therapy. Imagining breath being drawn down the spine and up the front of the body is a feature of traditional Chinese breathing techniques and is widely practised in meditation and the martial arts. Most people find that by visualising their breath as light or colour entering and circulating in the body they relax most effectively. Anne suffers from asthma and finds that breathing exercises normally make her tense because she thinks she will have an asthmatic attack. By imagining breathing in golden light she was able to relax very effectively. She explained that the imagery was so soothing and absorbing that it overcame her mental worries.

## Advantages of visualisation in relaxation

Including visualisation in relaxation procedures has several advantages: it promotes absorption, reduces reliance on verbal thinking and rational processes, and the tensions they generate. It also promotes insight into circumstantial, emotional and psychological factors underlying habitual bodily tensions which are normally unconscious.

### Reducing reliance on rational thinking
Nevertheless, initially at least, visualisation may not be sufficient to eliminate rational thinking altogether. Kath found it difficult to imagine her hands rising with the floor in the above exercise, because logically she realised that when seated in a chair her feet would rise first. Sue had similar thoughts but overcame them by imagining that she was lying on the floor rather than sitting in a chair, and that her hands and feet were rising simultane-

ously. If, like Kath, you found yourself unable to comply with the suggestions, it is because your head was getting in the way rather than your feet. That is, your logical verbal thinking processes were still overactive and need to be relaxed. If you are relaxed you won't give a thought to such logistical problems.

## Location of tensions

The location of tensions in the body varies from person to person depending on the ways in which they characteristically defend themselves against unpleasant experiences, and the extent of these. Nevertheless there do appear to be broad gender differences. Males appear to suppress problems by 'sitting' on them. Typically they describe the irritations, anxieties and concerns that give rise to their tensions as pains in the 'butt', 'bum', 'backside' or 'ass'. Female tensions seem to localise in the chest, however. Typically women need to 'get off their chest' whatever it is that 'gets on their tits', although they may prefer to keep them 'close to their chest'. When speaking of these issues they often place their hand on their chest (see pp. 105–6 and p. 124).

Of course, most of us are unaware not only of the location of our habitual tensions but also of the long-term physical consequences of these muscular patterns that can lead to weakness, debility and pain: to strain and breakdown.

# 4

# ASSESSING AND MANAGING STRESS

I live in a fairly remote house in the country with no near neighbours. It is accessed only by a long lane leading from a country road, from which it is not visible, and backs on to a large wood. Its sandstone walls are over a foot thick and so of necessity rather than choice the doorbell is particularly loud and strident. In the past ten years this bell has sounded only twice during the night, on both occasions when the milkman has reversed into the ditch running alongside the lane. I was therefore alarmed to be woken on another occasion at 4.30 a.m. by the bell, but with no milkman on the doorstep, and no sign of any lights, vehicle or person. While my husband conducted a search I lay in bed, tense from head to foot, my ears 'on stalks' listening for the slightest sounds, my breathing rapid and shallow. My mouth was dry and there seemed to be a lump in my throat. I felt an empty sensation that was almost but not quite 'butterflies' in my stomach. My mind was racing, turning again and again to the occasion two or three years previously when armed IRA terrorists burst into a farm less than a mile away demanding keys to the car in which they hoped to make their getaway after planting a bomb at the nearby army barracks. The more I thought of this incident the more tense and anxious I became. I was experiencing the classic symptoms of stress.

Half an hour later, when a thorough check of the house revealed a faulty fuse in the doorbell, I began to relax. My breathing slowed and steadied, the tensions in my muscles dissipated, removing the unpleasant sensations in my mouth, throat and stomach, and my anxiety was relieved. Within an hour I was asleep.

## The Physical Effects Of Stress

The term stress originates in a word meaning to tighten. This accurately describes the physical effects of reactions which prepare us either to avoid or confront potentially dangerous situations. These 'flight or fight' responses are the body's 'red alert' which prepares it to avoid potential injury and death. Irrespective of whether you confront or flee from danger the same bodily changes occur. Your muscles tense or tighten for action. The level of certain hormones rises, releasing stored sugars into the blood and increasing heart rate and blood pressure so that blood is forced to parts of the body needing it, and preparing the body for vigorous activity. Sugar and fats pour into the blood to provide energy for quick action. Chemicals are also released into the blood to enable it to clot rapidly in the event of injury. You breathe more rapidly to supply the muscles with oxygen, and perspire more in order to cool the body. These changes are experienced as 'butter-flies in the stomach', heart pounding, sweating, stiffness in various parts of the body especially the back and neck, tightness in the chest and a lump in the throat. Your body also places 'on hold' all processes not immediately essential to survival, so salivation and digestion cease, resulting in a dry mouth and an empty sensation in the stomach.

Once danger has passed the body quickly returns to normal. These responses are essential to health and survival. They are unhealthy only if they become habitual, and repeatedly triggered in response to non-threatening situations. The body then remains in a continually reactive state. Muscles stay tense, pulse rate and blood pressure remain increased, high levels of sugars, fats, cholesterol, hormones and other chemicals persist in the blood, and digestive processes are inactivated. Over time this state of dis-ease leads to the wear and tear of various body organs and takes its toll on health. It may result in cardiovascular problems, stroke, heart attack, kidney failure, diabetes, gastro-intestinal disorders and much else. Indeed it is estimated that 75 per cent of all medical complaints are stress-related. Many of these conditions are not merely inconvenient but can also be deadly.

Many people who are dis-eased in this way often do not realise it until clinical symptoms such as hypertension are diagnosed or they become ill. They have habituated to the symptoms of stress and for them such feelings are 'normal'. Not only are such people usually unaware that they are stressed but they often do not know what is stressing them. Shafa, a young man in his twenties, was surprised when his doctor informed him he was suffering from hypertension. It was months after the diagnosis when he was relaxing on a beach during a holiday that he realised how over-pressured he was by work. He decided to take it easy in future with the result that over a few months his blood pressure returned to normal. He realised that he also felt much less stressed than previously.

In some instances the symptoms of stress escalate quite dramatically, producing panic. Father Bernard, an elderly priest in a quiet rural parish, suffers from panic attacks which come upon him suddenly and unexpectedly in various situations such as when he is shopping. He has no doubt they are caused by stress and realises that his anxiety that they might occur adds to his overall level of stress and increases the likelihood that they will. Yet he has no idea why he is stressed.

## Stressors

Time, deadlines, being required to speak in public, noise, motorway driving and crowds are commonly identified as stressful. You may think that everyone experiences them in much the same way; that it is 'normal' to be stressed by them, and unavoidable, but this is not so. Many people would find it extremely stressful to be required to drink ten pints of fluid one after the other. Yet many people drink this amount of beer or lager in an evening and find it extremely pleasurable. They might be distressed if prevented from doing so. Similarly, some people find the idea of jumping from a bridge suspended only by a length of elastic quite horrifying while others consider it fun. It therefore makes little sense to regard specific events and circumstances as stressful in themselves.

It is more useful to think in terms of stressors – those events and circumstances that individuals *perceive* as stressful. Accordingly the stress associated with an event depends on how you view it. This is largely a matter of attitude. If you view an event negatively you will tend to experience it as unpleasant, and try to avoid it. You are likely to cope with it less well than someone who views it positively, as an opportunity to learn, grow and develop. If your attitude is habitually negative you are more likely to be continually stressed, and to succumb to stress-related illness. If you generally view events positively, as a challenge rather than a threat, you are likely not only to cope with them without experiencing stress and becoming ill, but you may also thrive on them. Avoiding these situations might prove more hazardous and stressful for you if, as a result, you became inert, understimulated and bored.

## Stress In The Imagination

The stress you experience not only depends on the way you see and think about the world – your attitude towards it – but also the beliefs you have about it. Many stressors reside wholly or partly within the imagination. Fears, anxieties and dread are often responses to our worst imaginings, rather than actual happenings, and many of them relate not to life-threatening or dangerous situations but to everyday, ordinary events. We may fear that no one likes us; that we will fail examinations or job interviews; that we will develop painful or debilitating illnesses; that our loved ones will be involved in accidents; and so on. It was not the door-bell ringing in the middle of the night that alarmed me but my imaginings about it. Had I imagined it was faulty I might have dismissed it, rolled over and gone back to sleep. If my imagination had been fuelled by a late-night horror or crime movie I had watched earlier I might have been even more alarmed and frightened.

Much of the stress we experience is undoubtedly a product of our imagination, determined by events, circumstances and things that are not externally real.

However, as indicated in chapter 3, the imagination also helps us to relax, lowering heart rate and blood pressure, decreasing breathing rate and producing an overall reduction in the speed of metabolism. As Exercise 3 will show, visualisation counteracts the harmful effects and uncomfortable feelings of stress. It also enables us to break free of 'worry cycles' – the tendency of the mind to play over and over again almost involuntarily the same anxieties and negative thoughts. Visualisation also provides insight into the attitudes, expectations, assumptions, thoughts and beliefs that underpin much stress. Visual images therefore often reveal hidden mental stressors of which you are normally unaware or unconscious, and reveal clues as to how you can alleviate and manage stress.

The following exercise is particularly effective in helping you to identify personal stressors. It also provides a way of managing stress by enabling you to relax.

## EXERCISE 3

### Managing Your Stress

Find somewhere you can sit with a reasonable degree of comfort. Close your eyes or focus with open eyes on a fixed point or object. Imagine that you have strings attached to your shoulders, arms and hands, and to the top of your head like a puppet, and that slowly and steadily these strings are being pulled, so that your head, shoulders, upper body, arms and hands are being drawn steadily upwards. Your spine is extending along its full length, your lower back arching and your thighs and legs flexing as you are pulled upwards. At the same time your chin is rising upwards and away from your neck, tilting backwards and then slightly forwards as your head raises.

Just as you begin to rise out of your seat the strings are cut and your body flops down on to the chair with your arms hanging by your sides. Focus for a few moments on the feelings of floppiness and allow them to spread throughout your body.

Having done so bring your attention to your chest. Imagine there a butterfly that is preparing to take flight. It seems more and more likely to do so each time you breathe in and out deeply, but remains there for some time without doing so. Observe it carefully, being aware of your feelings and thoughts as you do so. Note your reactions when eventually it takes flight.

Imagine following it to a pleasant situation where you feel relaxed, at ease, comfortable and secure. Pay careful attention to the sights, sounds, smells and sensations of this place; how it feels, and how you feel in it. Notice all the details of the scene as vividly as possible. Allow yourself to enjoy being there and to relax as fully as possible.

Having done so, ask yourself the following questions. What aspects of this imaginary situation do you find particularly restful or relaxing? What features of your everyday life are you getting away from in this situation? If this isn't clear, compare the imaginary situation with the usual situations of your everyday life. What might this imaginary exercise tell you about the stressors in your life?

When you have answered these questions remember that this imaginary place is always there for you to go. You carry it within yourself and can go there any time you wish.

Prepare to open your eyes and return your awareness to your surroundings. Now do so, and take a few moments to orientate yourself before recording the significant features of the exercise, including your answers to the above questions.

# Commentary

Many people, including those who usually find it difficult to relax or sleep, are astonished to find themselves relaxed, sometimes to the extent of 'drifting off' or falling asleep in response to the above exercise. Some 'come to' with little or no conscious recollection of parts of the exercise. Others describe experiencing pleasant 'woozy' sensations or 'drifting' in and out of ordinary conscious awareness much as though they are falling asleep.

## Common reactions

Most people find the experience pleasant and are reluctant to draw it to a conclusion. Helen imagined following a pure white butterfly into woodland where it disappeared among falling snowflakes which muffled all sounds. She felt totally relaxed and 'at one' with herself, suspended in a place where the only distinguishable sound was that of melting snowflakes. Like many others she was surprised to discover afterwards how long she had remained in this relaxed state. Certainly time appears to 'fly' when you are relaxed. If you normally experience time as a significant stressor relaxation will help to alleviate your stress. It may also help you to become aware of the effects of time-related stress.

Other common experiences reported in response to the

exercise are bodily sensations such as vibrations, waves, feelings of being suspended or very light; and mental states such as calmness, tranquillity and detachment. Tingling sensations or 'pins and needles' in limbs or body parts, loss of sensation and 'odd' sensations such as the arms being 'on the wrong way round' or the hands on different arms may also be experienced. These sensations may sometimes be alarming or experienced as unpleasant but they are entirely consistent with the physiological shifts that occur during relaxation and are a clear indication that the desired state is being achieved. Nevertheless they may prevent you progressing further with the exercise if you experience them. Chris was no longer able to continue when he became dizzy and anxious he would fall off his chair. Charlie was also jolted out of his relaxed state when he 'felt' his right arm fall off as he imagined the butterfly taking flight.

Some people find that as they begin to relax they encounter a residual anxiety, often quite unspecific, but sufficiently disturbing to prevent them sustaining the level of relaxation already achieved or progressing. This is because their habitual psychological and physical defences against anxiety and feelings that provoke anxiety are weakened. Some experience a spontaneous release of emotion as certain muscles relax. Sandra found herself crying for no obvious reason and only later realised that her tension protects her against feelings of hurt and sadness which might otherwise overwhelm her.

## Imagery preventing relaxation

As we have seen in the previous chapter, imagery promotes relaxation, but sometimes it prevents it. Kath, for example, imagined that she fell into many pieces when the strings supporting her were cut. She recognised that her fear of 'falling apart' and 'going to pieces' if she relaxed or 'let herself go' kept her tense. As a result she had great difficulty in relaxing and relinquishing her normal thought patterns. In contrast, Alison panicked when her normal thoughts were suspended and she imagined flying on the back of an elephant. She feared she was 'losing her mind', and this anxiety prevented her continuing with the exercise.

Intrusive and unpleasant images may also arise which generate anxiety and tension and prevent relaxation. These features need to be addressed, not simply because they prevent you relaxing but because they may reveal the unconscious fears, anxieties, concerns or memories which produce tension and may contribute to stress-related conditions. Diana felt quite distressed to see that her orange and white butterfly had large black spots which she interpreted as blemishes on her character. She hated everything about it and wanted to rid herself of it but could not. She saw in it her inability to accept herself as she is. It also made her realise how deeply ingrained her negative attitudes are, and the extent to which they create constant stress and anxiety in her life.

Sometimes the source of anxiety is being unable to imagine anywhere to feel relaxed, at ease or secure. Angela 'thought' she was relaxing in an imaginary garden until she was instructed to imagine somewhere she could be 'really' relaxed. When she realised she couldn't imagine such a place she became so anxious she was unable to proceed with the exercise. However, this experience enabled her to realise that she is not relaxed when she thinks she is and, more significantly, that this is because what she refers to as her 'mental computer' always remains active, telling her what she should and should not do. In this instance it directed her to go somewhere she could be 'really relaxed', implying that she wasn't 'doing' as well as she should in respect of both her imagination and relaxation. Her concern with 'doing' as she should, and doing it well, guarantees that she is never relaxed, even when she thinks she is, and needs to be abandoned in order for her to relax, 'really' and fully.

## Imaginary situations

Most people have little difficulty in imagining themselves in situations where they can relax, and these vary greatly. Some imagine themselves on beaches or in the sea, at favourite holiday resorts, in the mountains or other areas of natural beauty, or in more commonplace outdoor settings such as gardens, allotments, parks, canal banks and riversides. Others visualise themselves indoors in bed, the bath or comfortable chairs; watching animals, fish or birds; or engaging in a favourite pastime. These responses highlight the often overlooked benefits of leisure activities and pastimes, the natural environment and the companionship of animals.

Typically people are alone, with animals, or in situations where the other people present do not intrude on their physical or emotional space. Only rarely do they imagine being with children. This suggests that for many of us other people, particularly children, are a major stressor. On the face of it this seems something of a paradox, for we are social animals. However, it is not people per se that we need to distance ourselves from but their demands and expectations, specifically the requirement to 'be' and 'do' certain things.

## Identifying stressors

Domestic situations, relatives and children, and work are commonly identified as major stressors. Friends can also be stressors. Yvonne realised that in order to relax she had to get away from visitors 'dropping in' and from the telephone. Invasion of privacy is a significant stressor for many people, particularly teenagers and students, who find that their privacy is often invaded by parents and peers; and parents of young children who find they cannot even visit the bathroom without being disturbed.

Commonly, however, stressors are not specific people, circumstances or events but less tangible realities such as our own emotions. These are often highlighted by visualisation. Gloria imagined herself relaxing in a swimming pool, alone at 10.30 p.m., the time at which she normally completes her domestic chores. In this way Gloria realised she not only feels guilty if she hasn't fulfilled all these chores but also feels guilt because she resents having to fulfil the needs of others rather than her own. Similarly Jean, by imagining herself alone, realised that in order to relax she had to get away from the anger she feels towards others for expecting her to meet their needs while not respecting hers.

Pain may also be a source of stress. When Karen imagined herself lying in her garden at home she initially thought this meant that she was getting away from work. She could 'see' that she was quite unsettled, shifting about trying to find a comfortable position. She then realised that she was trying to avoid the pressure and pain of a long-standing neck injury. In so doing she became aware that she had become accustomed to the constant pain in her neck and was beginning not to notice it and the stress it caused her. It was therefore becoming an unconscious stressor. As a result of this insight she sought treatment for the condition, which proved to be effective.

The exercise may also highlight unmet needs which are a potential source of stress. Marilyn followed her imaginary butterfly deep into a dense jungle, and experienced a sense of great awe, calm and relaxation. It reminded her that she had not explored the remote areas of the places she had visited overseas as she had wanted to, or the deeper, inner areas of herself. She realised that her lack of initiative and adventurousness was an increasing source of frustration and that she needed to overcome these constraints in order to fulfil herself.

# 5

# IMPROVING YOUR
# SELF-AWARENESS

The stress management exercise in Chapter 4 highlights a paradox: we are social animals who need each other in order to survive. Yet we are stressed by each other to the extent that we often become ill, and may die, as a result. Most of us are rarely able to relax because of the constant pressure exerted by others as to how we should be and behave. This pressure is exerted even when other people are absent because we have internalised their demands and expectations since birth. These 'messages' are constantly relayed to us by our own thoughts, and there is no aspect of our existence that is not governed by them.

Talking about this subject at a workshop on a very hot summer's day, a group of men and women admitted that the demands and expectations of others made them uncomfortable – quite literally. Several of the women indicated that they would not show their pale, bare legs in public or wear 'skimpy' dresses because it is 'not the done thing'. Some admitted that they would not wear the clothes they might like to because they feared the adverse comments of others. Several men revealed that they never wore shorts because when they were young others had commented on their thin, spindly or bow legs. One who had been teased by being called 'chicken legs' said he would endure terrible heat before he would consider wearing shorts. Anxieties of this kind meant that most of this group of 30 adults tailored their appearance to the expectations of others, and restricted their activities to conform with them. So, on a hot day when they needed to be able to keep cool, many were suffering discomfort because they were over-dressed or reluctant to go for a swim and reveal their bodies.

## Self-denial

We often fail to meet our own needs because we are trying to meet the needs of others, or what we think, believe or imagine to be their needs. Denial of our needs, such as staying cool in hot weather, is undesirable and unhealthy. This self-denial inevitably creates tension and distress. It can also lead to illness because health depends on the fulfilment of all our needs – physical, psychological and spiritual. The problem for most of us is that we are so concerned with the needs of others that we pay insufficient attention to our own needs. We are not aware of them and so do not know what they are. In order to find out we have to distance ourselves from the messages in our minds that continually relay to us the needs of others.

In some ways our minds are like a television set broadcasting both sounds and pictures. Although we tend to assume that we 'watch' TV, much of the time we are only listening to the soundtrack while we read, knit, sew, prepare and eat meals, and engage in numerous other activities. It is only when the sound is turned down that we really need to look at the screen to gain some sense of what is happening. In much the same way our mind relays both pictures and sound simultaneously but we are so used to listening to the soundtrack – the continuous stream of verbal chatter in our heads – that we tend to ignore the pictures that are relayed by the mind's eye. We have little sense of them and we are, to all intents and purposes, oblivious to the complex information they convey. Only when we turn down the volume on the soundtrack – the 'shoulds', 'should nots', 'musts' and 'have tos' – can we 'see' what we need.

Visualisation enables us to 'switch off' our normal verbal thoughts and to gain insight into ourselves. It is therefore a valuable tool for self-awareness.

The following exercise promotes self-awareness by providing an insight into your needs.

## EXERCISE 4

### Promoting Self-awareness

Find somewhere you can sit comfortably. Having done so, close your eyes or focus on a fixed point. Imagine you are sitting outdoors on a warm, sunny day. The heat from the sun is pleasant rather than oppressive and you can feel its rays warming but not burning your body. As you become aware of your body and the sensations within it you identify areas of tension, discomfort or pain. You imagine these in the form of ice. As you focus attention on each of these areas in turn you imagine that the sun's rays are penetrating your body and melting the ice. Your tensions, discomfort and pains dissolve, first into a trickle and then into a stream of warm water which flows through and out of you leaving your body feeling warm and heavy.

When your bodily tensions have disappeared focus on your head. Imagine that the sun's rays are penetrating into your mind and dissolving your mental tensions and anxieties. They too flow away through and out of your body, leaving your mind clear.

Now imagine a flowering plant. Observe it carefully. Notice its situation and surroundings. Pay close attention to its flowering and fruiting parts, noting their number, colour, quality and condition. Observe also the leaves, their number, colour, quality and condition; and the branches and stems of the plant.

Follow the stems downwards noting their features. Notice how many there are and their appearance. Note how they enter into the medium in which the plant is growing. Follow the stem into the medium and see how it emerges from the roots. Follow the roots and observe them closely, noting their features. Are they deep or shallow, short or extensive? Do they encounter any obstacles? How well do they support the plant?

Now pay attention to the medium the roots are in. Note the nature, colour, texture and quality of this medium. Having done so attend once more to the roots. Follow them upwards to the surface, noting how the plant emerges from it. Then follow the stem upwards to its full height. Notice the outlook of the plant. Then withdraw from it so you can view it from a distance. As you do so identify what this plant needs in order to be fully healthy and to bring its potentials to fruition. Having done so ask yourself what this plant reveals about you, its creator; and about what you need in order to be fully healthy and to bring your potentials to fruition.

When you have answered these questions allow the image to fade. Return to ordinary awareness and record your experiences, including your answers to the questions.

## Commentary

A flowering plant presents an image which is simultaneously simple and complex. Few people have difficulty imagining such a plant, and where they do this usually indicates resistance. Some people are aware of consciously trying to change or modify the plant they first imagine. This usually occurs when they do not want to acknowledge or accept some aspect of the image that arises spontaneously. They invariably find that the original image resists all attempts to change it and obliges them to pay attention to it. If you wished to change or found it hard to accept the plant you imagined, or any part of it, pay close attention to these features. They probably represent repressed aspects of yourself and may have important implications for your overall well-being.

The image of a flowering plant is complex because it is a natural, dynamic, organic entity that grows and develops and is sensitive to environmental factors. For this reason it features in traditional symbolism throughout the world and typically represents the development of the whole person rather than any one part. Philosophers and teachers often draw analogies between plants and people at various levels, and Christ frequently did so in his parables. The image of a flowering plant enables us to represent many features of ourselves in a novel way, including those aspects of which we are normally unaware or unconscious. In this way it helps to provide new insights and different perspectives on issues.

## Nature of the plant

The nature of the plant may reveal the way you see yourself, and other important features of your character. Chloe imagined a mechanical dancing flower in a pot. She dismissed it as silly and later realised that she doesn't take herself seriously and doesn't expect other people to. She therefore has little faith in herself and takes little or no notice of her own ideas or intuition. The image also revealed an insecure background to which she attributed much of her lack of confidence in herself. Wendy imagined a pink rose that was depicted on the playing cards she remembered from childhood. The rose was perfect but unreal with 'gentle little thorns that wouldn't hurt anyone'. She realised it highlighted the conflict she experiences between being the perfect gentle, unaggressive, unassertive girl she was taught to be as a child and the real person she wishes to be as a woman. After the exercise she wrote, 'An understanding I gained from this image was that the rose was harmless, artificial, flat, had no real perfume and no real life of its own. I drew from this the notion of myself as ineffectual in many situations, giving a false account of my thoughts and feelings on many occasions, no strong personality, never prepared to "cause a stink" to bring about change or make my feelings known. Operating on such a self-deceptive front may cause less embarrassment and hurt to others and self but is ultimately unfruitful in that there is no genuine exchange of ideas and emotions and no real growth as a consequence'. She 'really' needs to grow.

## Situation of the plant

The overall context or atmosphere in which the plant is situated may reveal the way you view the situation in which you find yourself, and your outlook on life. This may be positive or negative. For example a marsh marigold or other wetland plant may reveal that a person is 'bogged down' or 'swamped' in some way. One man who described his plant as 'waterlogged' began to cry as he did so. Kath imagined a geranium planted in a pot outdoors, sheltered by a house from the slight chill in the air. She realised that the image reflects the basic tension in her life between being restricted and confined on the one hand and yet being unable to move far from the protection of her home. Bob imagined a healthy bush with red flowers but could not name it. He saw this as an indication that while he has a very clear idea of himself he can't express his true nature to others. Tom could not identify the plant he imagined and admitted that he has no clear sense of his identity. This plant, in a small pot on a patch of ground outside a house, looked 'OK' from a distance but torn and 'tatty' at close quarters. To Tom it revealed the restriction he feels living at home with his parents when he had expected to move away, and also his sense of being in transition, unsettled and insecure. Sarah interpreted the absence of other flowers near the plant she imagined as an indication that she lacks stimulation and needs more interest in some areas of her life.

## The flowering and fruiting parts

The flowering and fruiting parts of the plant may suggest the extent to which your potentials have flowered or borne fruit; those aspects of yourself that have yet to come to fruition; or those that have been 'nipped in the bud'. Many people see that their budding powers, potentials and ambitions have not been realised, or have yet to emerge. By contrast Yvonne imagined a cactus-like plant with pink flowers which were growing bigger and bigger. She felt anxious that this blossom might overpower the plant, and realised that like it she needed more space in which to grow and allow her potentials to develop fully.

## Features of the flowers and leaves

The colour, shape and number of the flowers and their condition may also be significant, as might the specific features of the leaves. Paul said of his plant that 'the rot has set in at the top'. Its flowers were all brown and their petals falling. He realised that this revealed his disenchantment with his career. Shafa who imagined experimenting with his plant by subjecting it to various weather conditions such as snow, heavy rain, high winds and thunder, realised that much of the stress he had suffered in the past was because he had always been testing himself by presenting unnecessary challenges. He imagined the physical condition that resulted from the stress he had created for himself as a fungal infection which extended from the flowers to the roots of the plant. This receded, allowing the plant to 'pick itself up again' when the weather conditions were more settled. In this way he realised that he should not expose himself to stress by pushing himself to his limits.

Leaves often relate to those features of yourself or your life you have been obliged to leave or suppress in order to conform to the demands and wishes of others. They often highlight neglected qualities that have not been paid sufficient attention. They may also indicate features that you may have to leave or forgo in order to achieve your potential and to express yourself fully. Richard identified them as the first things that he 'leaves out' or lets go of in difficult situations. For Mark the magnolia tree he imagined in full bloom was without leaves because of the many things he had dropped, quite deliberately, in order to express his homosexuality and realise himself. John suggested that, like the evergreen holly bush he imagined, he cannot be without his defences, although his 'prickliness' often prevents him expressing his true feelings. Upon imagining a plant densely covered with leaves the phrase 'leave well alone' came to Sue's mind. Like Richard she saw them as having a defensive/protective function.

## The stems

The stems may provide some indication of how much support or strength you see yourself possessing. Mary interpreted the firm stem of the plant she imagined as an indication that she was 'standing up' well under her present circumstances, and coping. Some people see the straight stems they imagine as an indication of their rigidity or stubbornness, and single stems are often seen as a sign of single-mindedness. There may be a good deal of dead wood, or new growth, various entanglements, restrictions, or undergrowth that may reveal the order, confusion or chaos in your life. In this way you may be able to identify where some of the stress in your life 'stems' from. Woody growth and thorns may reflect your defences and provide some idea of the threats to your well-being you perceive, albeit unconsciously. The heavily flower-laden wisteria Jane imagined needed the firm support of a wall until its stem grew into a substantial trunk.

## Growth medium

The growth medium of the plant may provide some insight into the culture in which you have been reared, particularly your family culture and early environment. The roots suggest how secure or well-grounded you are in that culture and may highlight obstacles to growth and development that you were presented with, together with ways in which you coped with them. Gloria imagined a flower with only a short stem, cut off from its roots and suspended in space. She realised that this reflects not only that she is cut off from her childhood and is not nourished emotionally by it, but also the way she remains in suspense by putting off any major emotional involvement in her life. Julie imagined a bunch of daffodils in a clear glass vase outside on a stone wall in the garden of the cottage she had lived in as a child. The tips of the daffodil stems were brown where they had 'bled' from being cut. She saw this as an indication of her sense of hurt at being cut off from her roots, her childhood and her home, and her vulnerability. Dennis's roots growing down through cliffs reflected his sense of having a firm foothold in something enduring and solid.

The way in which the plant emerges from the growth medium may also reveal the ease or difficulty with which you emerged from your early environment into the wider world, and the effects of that transition on your later development. Justin imagined his plant emerging in the middle of a football field where a game was in progress. Not surprisingly perhaps, his experience of early school-ing was of one painful 'put down' after another.

## 'Seeing' your needs

You may find that this exercise affords profound insight into yourself and into your needs. Mark realised that while the leafless appearance of his magnolia tree fully exposed its flowers they nevertheless had the appearance of being 'out on a limb'. He realised that it needed only one person sitting under it to achieve a sense of balance and harmony. Chris imagined a sunflower which needed water desperately, with a pixie among its roots. Initially she had no idea what the pixie represented. She was more concerned that she might need water and for a few days carried a bottle of mineral water with her until she realised that the lack of water represented her emotional needs. The pixie had been so busy cleaning and dusting the tunnels within the roots that it had paid no attention to their water supply, and in much the same way she had been so preoccupied with the needs of her family that she had neglected her own.

Sandra imagined what she thought was a sunflower seed planted in a first-class compost. However, the seed received insufficient water and when the plant blossomed it produced a violet sweet pea. Standing alone and unsup-ported it didn't 'look right'. Indeed it leaned to the left. Sandra thought it needed 'a bit of string to hold its head up'. She felt disappointed to have imagined such a pale, delicate and insignificant flower instead of a big, strong, bright and noticeable sunflower, and admitted that when she saw the sweet pea she felt 'something akin to embar-rassment'. Discussing her imagery with friends helped her to realise that the soil represented her childhood experiences. Her father had always been uncomfortable with emotion and she had been obliged to suppress her emotions and her natural inclinations. He often referred to her as 'soft in the head'. He had also been dismissive of her interests and she felt that in his affections she didn't match up to her brother who shared her father's technical and mathematical abilities. She realised she had struggled all her life to compete with her brother and to appear clever enough to gain her father's approval. Her imagery therefore reflected her desire to 'do right' in her father's eyes and measure up intellectually, and also her failure to stand up for herself and her interests. She also realised that the violet flower symbolised her interest in astrology. This imagery gave her insight into her needs and the determination to pursue her interests more openly, with less concern about the opinions of others.

When you begin to 'see' your needs in this way you are more likely to pay greater attention to them.

# 6

## CONTROLLING
## YOUR LIFE

Throughout childhood we are taught to 'do as you are told'. We all learn the unpleasant and sometimes painful consequences of not doing so. We therefore try to gain and maintain the approval of others in order to avoid punishment. This often means suppressing rather than expressing ourselves and denying what we want to do in favour of what others expect and demand.

### Giving Away Control

Because we tend to value ourselves as we are valued by others their approval normally serves to increase our self-esteem. Therefore our assessment of how others react towards us influences our view of ourselves. If the assessment appears favourable we are likely to develop a positive view of ourselves and our worth, and self-confidence. If it appears unfavourable we are likely to feel bad about ourselves and lack self-esteem. We may try to adjust our behaviour to the requirements of others by suppressing those aspects of ourselves that generally don't find favour and expressing those that do. While this may not attract hostility it is likely to result in blandness and superficiality.

Each of us gives away control over ourself to others to the extent that we rely on their confirmation, endorsement or validation of our thoughts, feelings, actions, beliefs and opinions. This means that others have authority and power over us, and that we are not fully in control of ourselves and our lives. Many of us compulsively give authority away to others by always looking to them for approval, advice and guidance rather than listening to ourselves. We respect others rather than ourselves, and therefore listen to and trust them, even though they are often in no better position themselves to judge. Ironically, therefore we respect and listen to people who do not respect or listen to themselves.

Over-reliance on the approval of others produces an exaggerated concern for outward appearances, and inauthenticity. It leads to feelings of being controlled by others rather than oneself. Those who lack a sense of being in control of their lives are likely to think more negatively about themselves, to feel more inadequate, less confident and happy than those who perceive themselves as having control. They are less likely to express emotion than those who feel in control but more likely to experience high levels of anxiety and to be depressed more often. Their attempts to gain the approval of everyone are likely to result in conflict, confusion and tension, so they are likely to experience more stress than those who express themselves more authentically. They generally respond less well to stress because events they perceive as stressful invariably pose a direct challenge to their personal control.

## The Cost Of Suppression

Shaping our expression and behaviour to the requirements of others may avoid their condemnation, but it is not without cost. As we have seen, constantly adjusting to the requirements and demands of others invariably leads us to deny our needs and fail to express them. If we are unaware of our needs we are unable to satisfy them and this can lead to illness. Research has shown that emotionally inexpressive people are 16 times more likely to develop cancers than those who feel their emotions intensely and express them. Cancer patients are typically bland, stoic, self-denying, repressed and strongly conformist. They are likely to say that all is well with them when it is not. They are also likely to have experienced feelings of loss and depression before the onset of their disease.

Those who repress, suppress or depress themselves may from time to time assert themselves, sometimes in outbursts of aggression, against those to whom they strive too closely to conform. However, afterwards they revert to their habitual approval-seeking, and often feel guilty about their earlier lapse in behaviour. The suppression of anger and guilt therefore tends to be significantly associated with feelings of helplessness, and with cancer.

Reliance on the approval of others in order to maintain self-esteem or feelings of worth is also damaging to mental health. Those who do so are much more prone to despair and depression if anything goes wrong, and therefore more vulnerable than those who have an inner source of self-esteem. They are more likely to see themselves as unable to control events and helpless, and so are more likely to succumb to mental illness, morbidity, clinical depression, anxiety and adverse stress conditions. They are also more likely to attempt or commit suicide.

# Following The Wrong Messages

Much depression is a consequence of the messages that guide people's lives. These are provided by others and the wider society, and once learned and internalised they remain largely unquestioned and unchanged. These messages spring unbidden to the mind when certain situations arise and serve as guiding rules of conduct: 'I shouldn't show my feelings'; 'I must not cry'; 'I must be strong'; 'I mustn't show anger, I should be calm'; 'I should not offend others'; 'I must not speak my mind'. Warnings such as this which have been instilled in the past, and added to continually, often have little of relevance to the present, but they remain firmly in mind nevertheless, as a reminder of what we should say, do and feel. If we listen to and follow them these messages can impose severe restrictions on us, prevent us taking control of our lives or changing.

Most of us don't consider ourselves worth listening to and this determines the extent to which we are in control of and have authority over our lives. Failure to listen to your own knowledge and to follow your own advice and instructions – literally your intuitions or inner teaching – leads to disempowerment and disease. Many of those who suffer from serious illnesses such as coronary heart disease typically ignore or undervalue their intuition, and cancer patients may have become completely cut off from their inner resources. Certainly many of those who have recovered from such conditions view their illness as, in part, a message to pay more attention to their unconscious self and its needs rather than the demands of others.

Those who rely on the messages of others as guides to their behaviour, attitudes and values, and to provide meaning, often find that at various stages in life this guidance fails. They don't answer the questions and so no longer provide meaning as they have done formerly. Such crises frequently result in disappointment and pain, but they actually present a valuable opportunity for us to re-evaluate these messages and the roles and ways of being they relate to, and to let go of these where necessary. The disorientation they produce is necessary because if we are not disappointed or let down by the outside voices of our lives we will not let go of them and will hang on to what is familiar even though it doesn't work for us any more and creates depression and poor health.

However, many of us do not use such crises or the pain and suffering they produce as messages to reappraise and let go of those aspects of life that are no longer meaningful or of value to us. We continue to live our lives by outdated messages acquired in our past and to hold on to outmoded roles, relationships, behaviours, attitudes, beliefs and feelings they dictate, and the pain and hurt they generate.

It is not necessary to experience illness or crisis in order to let go of the control that others have over you through the messages you have learned to rehearse and obey. The first stage in initiating self-control is to listen to yourself and recognise your authority. This can be achieved through visualisation. The following exercise will help you to make contact with and establish communication with your inner teacher, your intuition.


## EXERCISE 5

### Contacting Your Inner Teacher

Find somewhere to sit comfortably and close your eyes or focus your open eyes on a fixed point or object. Having done so begin silently counting backwards from 300. Do not attend to distracting thoughts. Be aware of them but do not hold on to them, and return your attention to counting downwards, matching your breathing with your counting. With each out breath let go of a little of the tension in your body so that you become progressively more and more relaxed.

Imagine that as you count downwards you are descending steps. The steps are steep and you pause on each one to breathe in deeply before moving down on the next as you breathe out. As you slowly descend the steps you become aware of feeling tired and heavy. You pause for a moment and as you do so you see a person coming up the steps towards you. As the person gets nearer you realise it is yourself. Note your feelings and thoughts as you see yourself, and also details of your appearance, dress, facial expression and manner.

As you get closer still take the opportunity to speak to yourself. Be aware of how you feel about doing so, and how your other self responds as you try to engage it in conversation. Listen carefully to what, if anything, your other self says to you, and take note of anything it communicates in any other way. Be aware of your impressions and feelings as you do so. If you are able to, arrange a convenient time and place to meet in future before you part. Having done so, continue on your way. Allow the image to fade and return to normal awareness.

Take time to record your experience and any insights derived from it. Pay close attention to any communication between yourself and your double, noting any messages, information or advice conveyed by the latter, and your reactions.

# Commentary

## *Common reactions*

Reactions to meeting the other self on the stairs are very mixed. Most people are quite surprised, even shocked, to meet themselves, but most react favourably to the encounter. Many people are surprised by the energy and vitality of their other self. Some see themselves as more vivacious, attractive, energetic, carefree, determined and youthful, even childlike. Often simply seeing themselves in this way is sufficient to make them aware of aspects of themselves they have 'lost touch' with. Janet imagined descending the stone steps of her grandmother's cellar and meeting herself as a child of about six or seven dressed in clothes she used to 'dress up' in at that age, and holding a kitten in her arms. She was startled to find that when she spoke to the child, asking her what she was doing there, her tone was abrupt. The child replied that she was going to put the kitten in the orchard and pick flowers for her grandmother. This brief encounter affected Janet profoundly. She felt that she was no longer in touch with this child-self, which represented something she was losing sight of as a result of the pressures and tensions of her present and uncertainties about her future. She described this as her 'most pure and true self, happy and cheerful. The essence of who I really am'. She realised she had lost the carefree but caring attitude she had as a child, and that the message of the imagery was twofold: not to be so serious about life; and to acknowledge and honour the importance of her grandmother, now dead.

Occasionally people see themselves as older, more mature, wise and serene. In addition to the wise counsel so often communicated by their older selves, they may also confront their fears about growing old and realise that many of their anxieties are unfounded. Very commonly the advice they receive is to live fully in the present rather than worrying about the future or regretting the past.

Usually, however, people encounter their double. It may look exactly like them physically and wear the same clothes. Nevertheless differences in their manner or facial expression often communicate a great deal. David, a rather 'hot-headed' teenager whose aggression was creating numerous problems for him, met himself coming up the stairs in an underground cavern wearing torn blue jeans and long hair like himself. He thought his double looked 'cool' but rather cold. He therefore told his double that it was really hot upstairs, but, thinking that it might be good to cool down, arranged to meet him later by an ice-cream kiosk after he had visited the cavern. Afterwards he realised that his double was showing him how to cool down, stay cool and be 'cool'.

Angela was very aware that when she was descending the steps she was looking down and concentrating very carefully on where she placed her feet and was holding on to a bannister for support, whereas her other self, while exactly the same physically, climbed upstairs in an easy, relaxed manner, looking upwards and with a smile on her face. What she termed the 'down self' was surrounded by a dark light, whereas the 'up self' was walking in front of a warm orange light. Angela realised that her confident, outgoing, cheerful self was showing her that she need not be so diffident, careful and reliant on external support.

## Advice from the double

The advice or information given by the double may be profound, or it may seem trivial. However the most simple communications are often extremely poignant. Rosie gained great comfort from her double when it touched her gently and said 'You're OK'. Kevin was told to go and get himself something to eat rather than do the work he planned to. Initially he thought this referred to the way he was neglecting himself physically because of his work. He realised later that because of his obsession with work he had also neglected to 'feed' himself emotionally and spiritually.

Ahmed imagined descending a metal stairway but although he could see through the rungs he couldn't see the bottom of the stairs because they were in total darkness. Suddenly his double emerged from the dark with a big grin on his face and told him as he passed 'Don't worry. You won't be here much longer'. When Ahmed turned to see him he was waving and smiling, and so Ahmed followed him upstairs, at ease and smiling also. This simple exchange was very meaningful to Ahmed who was stressed and depressed to be working overseas. His double reminded him that the situation was only temporary and that he could be more positive about it rather than let it get him down. Jackie also chose to follow her double whose cheery reply to the question 'Where are you going?' was simply 'Up. It's sunnier.'

## Communicating with the self

Many people do not recognise the self they meet on the steps, and this often shows them that they are out of touch with themselves. Some have a strong feeling that it is them but don't recognise it as such. Others recognise themselves but feel awkward or uncomfortable and don't know what to say. They may want to speak but don't have the courage to do so. Initiating conversation may be difficult. They may shake hands rather formally, as they might with a stranger, or ask 'How are you?' or 'How are you doing?' Ted felt embarrassed when, having greeted his double, he had no idea what to say because he didn't know him. Some people panic as they realise that they may miss an opportunity to establish contact with themselves.

If conversation occurs it may be stilted. Some people find their attempts to engage their double in conversation fail. This may be because their manner is aggressive or challenging. They may be also see their stony faces, aloofness, coldness, 'shortness', 'sharpness', harshness, and such like. In this way you may gain insight into how you appear to others and why they respond to you as they do. It may be the double that speaks first, in which case you might find it useful to consider the extent to which you show initiative and take control of and responsibility for situations.

## Strangers to our selves

Some people don't want to talk or even attempt to initiate conversation. They may stare at themselves or feel 'shifty', avert their eyes and walk on. One woman described being relieved to get to the bottom of the stairs. If you react in this way to your encounter you might find it useful to consider how you and your self have become strangers, and what you need to do to become friends.

Julie gained insight into her self-alienation when she imagined being unable to find herself and able only to *hear others* when she descended the steps in a castle. Ellen saw herself only fleetingly, like a ghost, and like others who see themselves only as a 'ghostly presence', realised that that this indicated her lack of self-awareness and insight. Some people are quite alarmed to glimpse themselves only briefly. Brenda realised she hadn't seen herself for years.

Sometimes it is fear or dislike of those normally hidden aspects of themselves that prevent communication. Many people believe that these features of themselves are undesirable and best avoided. Mark didn't trust the other self he met on the stairs. One young woman who described being frightened descending the stairs in the dark indicated that this may be because she feels able 'to shed little light on herself'. She sensed her other self near her but would not speak to it because she preferred to remain in the dark about this unknown and frightening aspect of herself. Sue was also disturbed by her image, not because it was unpleasant. On the contrary, it was a cheerful, open character but Sue sensed another presence – a 'lurking, silent, cheerless, drab self' that she didn't feel happy about. She didn't want to acknowledge this aspect of herself, because it conflicted with her 'image' of how she wanted to be, but it would not go away. She recognised the outfit it was wearing as one she had once possessed but 'now did not own'. She realised that the disturbing image represented the disowned parts of herself, those she represses because she doesn't feel strong enough to deal with them at present.

Clearly, many people are not at ease with themselves and they don't want, or don't feel able, to reconcile their different aspects. They prefer to remain strangers. Rather fewer people know themselves well and fewer still are very comfortable with themselves. Others are surprised to find that they like themselves and to discover how well they get along together. 'It's almost as though I have a good friend in myself', said Pat. Some do not want to part. They are determined to remain friends, to stay in touch and to listen to themselves.

# 7

## ALLEVIATING
## DISEASE

A correspondence can often be found between the language we use, and the physical illnesses and symptoms we experience. Gloria, for instance, characteristically prefaces an explanation of the irritations in her life by saying 'what sticks in my throat' or 'what chokes me off'. She experiences a lump in her throat when she is anxious, and suffers repeatedly from throat infections and problems. Christine, who described herself as 'busting a gut' to move house, afterwards suffered a severe intestinal disorder. Marty suffers from repeated intestinal complaints. She typically responds to emotional upset by claiming she is 'gutted', and describes annoyances and frustrations as 'gut wrenching'. Sandra, who is always saying that things 'get up her nose' is never without a decongestant spray for her chronic sinus and catarrh. Tony finds many situations 'a bummer'. He suffers from haemorrhoids. Joe is 'livid' about various events in his life. He suffers from a rare form of skin cancer whose major symptoms are redness and severe irritation. Pat finds many of the aspects of her life a 'bleeding nuisance'. She needed a hysterectomy to prevent continual haemorrhaging. Jane who was 'fed up to the back teeth' with her job, underwent lengthy and unsuccessful dental examinations to try and establish the cause of the pain in her rear molars. Anne who repeatedly declared she could no longer deal with the 'shit' in her life, was rushed into hospital suffering with a blocked bowel; and John, who was 'galled' to have to take early retirement, developed gallstones soon afterwards, having never previously been ill in his life. Given these correspondences, and the many more I have encountered, I was very concerned to hear a young woman declare that she was 'titsed off' with life.

## 'Target' Areas

It seems that the bodily images suggested by the figures of speech we habitually use relate in some way to the physical symptoms we develop. Figures of speech may therefore be a reliable indictor of actual or potential health problems. Although there is no proof that this is so, there is evidence to suggest that certain emotional tensions tend to afflict certain parts of the body just as certain pathological micro-organisms are known to have an affinity for specific organs. These 'target' organs or parts of the body with special significance to the tensions in our lives are the most likely areas for disease to take root. The surgeon Bernie Siegel believes that we sensitise these target areas quite unconsciously through our use of verbal imagery. We are therefore unaware that our minds affect our bodies in this way. Barbara Hoberman Levine also insists that 'your body believes every word you say' in her book of this title.

If this is the case we need to pay close attention to the language we habitually use to describe our responses to and feelings about events. If you can relate the language you most commonly use with the tensions and pains in various parts of your body, or the illnesses you most frequently develop, you need to avoid using these phrases. It is perhaps a good idea to avoid using any figures of speech that convey body images.

However, if your body does believe every word you say then it makes sense to use this principle to bring about desired effects. You can, for example, deliberately 'target' specific muscles and body parts by focusing attention on them and telling them to relax. This is a fundamental principle of autogenic training, a very effective relaxation procedure developed in the 1930s by an eminent neurologist and now widely used within medicine in the management and treatment of many medical conditions.

Autogenic training uses visualisation to bring about initial relaxation in various ways. For example, one technique uses elements similar to those included in Exercise 3 (Managing Your Stress, p. 70). It advises you to sit on the edge of a straight-backed chair so that only your buttocks are on the seat and your thighs touching it only slightly, and with your feet positioned so that the heel of one foot is directly aligned with the toes of the other. You are then instructed to imagine a string from the top of your head to the ceiling which is pulling you into an upright position with both arms hanging at your side. You then imagine that the string is cut so that your head flops forward like a rag doll. This usually results in a vertical collapse of the trunk, shoulders and neck into a relaxed posture, but it is very important that you don't collapse into such a concave posture that your breathing becomes difficult.

In this relaxed mode the first series of exercises

commences. Attention is first directed to each arm in turn. While attending to this arm repeat silently to yourself 'My right (or left) arm is heavy' 3–6 times for 30–60 seconds. Then flex the arm energetically, breathe deeply and open your eyes while repeating the 'cancellation' formula 'arms firm, breathe deeply, open eyes'. Repeat this exercise four times. Having done so focus attention on your other arm and proceed as previously. Then repeat the exercise focusing on both arms together.

The second stage involves telling the arms, and subsequently the other limbs, that they are warm. In further exercises you repeat the phrases 'heart beat calm and regular', 'it breathes me', 'my solar plexus is warm' and 'my forehead is cool' in order to regulate the heart, reduce your rate of respiration, induce calming of the central nervous system and keep a cool head.

After a variable period of training you should be able to complete the exercises in a few minutes and maintain a state – known as the autogenic state – of relaxation for prolonged periods.

A more simple and less time consuming way of achieving desired physical effects is to picture them directly rather than convey them in words. So, for example, you can relax tensions in your arms and chest by first imagining gripping a coin, as in Exercise 2a (p. 58) and then releasing it, or release tensions in other muscles by imagining that a rising floor you are resisting falls away. You can reduce your rate of breathing by imagining a butterfly drying its wings on your chest as in Exercise 3 (p. 71). You can promote generalised bodily relaxation or the relaxation of specific muscles by imagining their tension in the form of ice being dissolved away by the warming rays of the sun, as in Exercise 4 (p. 81).

Although as presented in these exercises the recommended images are used to relax muscle tension, they may also be used to aid muscle tightening, and therefore can be used to strengthen weak muscles and ligaments. Mental rehearsal using images in this way can be used not only in rehabilitation following injury but also in training of physical skills to improve performance. For example, the discovery that muscle tension increases in persons who imagine lifting progressively heavy weights has been incorporated into the training of some athletes and in fitness programmes. Similarly the awareness that heart rate can be increased by imagining running is widely applied by sports scientists. It is also possible to increase internal blood flow or decrease external bleeding by way of vivid images. As indicated in Chapter 1, visualisation is recognised as having an important role in effecting positive physiological changes, including improvement of immune function. It can therefore influence the course of disease. Visualisation may also be used as a way of confronting fears and feelings of hopelessness and helplessness, enabling you to gain a sense of control and a change in negative attitudes. It also allows you to communicate with your unconscious mind where unhealthy beliefs may be hidden, and may provide valuable insights into your physical condition.

The following exercise will help you to establish communication with and gain insight into the processes of your body, and to promote effective healing.


## EXERCISE 6

### Communicating with Your Body Processes

**Find somewhere to sit comfortably with your eyes closed or focused on a fixed point. Imagine you are**

sitting in front of a warm fire. You can smell and hear it, and feel its warmth on your face and body. As you watch the flames flickering your tensions, aches and pains gradually dissolve so that you become more and more relaxed. Allow yourself to enjoy relaxing in this way for several minutes.

Having done so, become aware of any areas of tension, pain or discomfort that remain in your body. Focus your attention on the least comfortable area and imagine a replica of yourself shrinking smaller and smaller so that it can enter your body through the pores of your skin. Imagine it going into your body and conducting a full and thorough investigation of that area. Establish what is happening there, and what is needed to improve the situation. Try to avoid thinking of biological or anatomical details. Simply allow images and impressions to form spontaneously, and do not censor them in any way.

You may find it useful to talk to and interact with the features you encounter so as to gain as full a picture of the situation as possible.

When you are satisfied that you have investigated the area fully and formed some idea of what is needed, relay this information to your body's healing forces, wherever they are situated, and direct them to deal with it in any way that seems appropriate.

Imagine this in as much detail as possible, noting the location and appearance of your healing forces and how responsive or otherwise they appear. Supervise them as they tackle the problem. Observe how they do so, and how satisfactorily. Insist on the highest standards of work and that the area is left clean and tidy on its completion. If the job cannot be cannot be dealt with immediately negotiate a programme of work to be carried out, and agree a time scale for its completion. Make it clear that you will return from time to time to monitor progress. When this is agreed leave the healing forces to work and return to the surface of your body. Note any changes that you experience in your body. Then allow yourself to return to normal awareness, and take some time to record your experience.

## Commentary

For most people this is a very enjoyable, and often amusing exercise. It may also be very surprising. The area where most discomfort is experienced might be quite different to what was expected. Julia discovered pain and tension in areas she had not previously recognised. These were not being treated during the physiotherapy treatment she was receiving because she believed the pain was confined to her back.

### Common imagery

The areas of pain, tension and discomfort are not usually 'seen' as physical organs and tissue. You may have pictured thickened tubes, tightened ligaments, seized-up joints and retained fluid if you know these are features of your medical condition. Shafa visualised constricted arteries and himself flying along inside them with his arms outstretched sideways. He also began to see the pressure he felt in his chest as a fog which he could guide out of his body with a hand. Clearly by way of visualisation he was giving himself a hand in more ways than one.

You are more likely to have imagined very non-anatomical features such as walls, masonry or piles of rubble; sooty tunnels and grimy underground railway platforms; sewers, scaffolding, rusting metalwork, leaking pipes and broken or dysfunctional equipment of various kinds. You may have imagined one or more persons. Shirley sees and refers to the arthritis she has suffered since childhood as 'Arfur', a temperamental little man who 'flares up' when she is under pressure. You may have seen an animal, like Mike who saw a rat, or animals, like Ann who pictured a number of mice. You may have imagined a plant, like June, whose poison ivy was out of control.

You may have imagined your body's healing forces as biological cells, but you are more likely to have seen them as little men in white suits or blue coveralls, wearing helmets and equipped with various machines, hi-tech gadgetry, transportation and weaponry; soldiers, ancient or modern; sailors; firefighters; painters, decorators, plumbers, plasterers, fitters, electricians, mechanics, engineers, gardeners, miners or space travellers. They may have appeared on bicycles, in boats, cars, lorries, fire-engines, various aircraft, space ships or on foot.

Armed variously with shovels, picks, hammers, power drills and hoses, water cannon, paint stripper, vacuum suction devices, haulage, construction or demolition equipment – anything and everything appropriate to the task in hand, they streamline, automate, deactivate and rationalise various physical functions.

Or you may have imagined an 'army' of cleaners equipped with buckets, brushes and every conceivable cleaning aid; seamstresses, or maids with smoothing irons. You may have pictured these workers striving to hammer, chisel, oil and lubricate stiff joints; to release tightened screws and vices; demolish or blast away obstructions and blockages; 'declog' or scour veins and arteries; pump or drain away excess fluid; remove dust, dirt, grime and debris; smooth muscles; repair cuts and tears; sanitise and fumigate.

You may have imagined other forces at work, such as light, lasers, sunshine, infra-red rays, other kinds of radiation, soundwaves, music, worker bees or ants, sniffer dogs or minesweepers.

## Insights into bodily functions

This imagery may give you important insights into the effectiveness of your body's healing processes. The activities you picture may be well organised or totally chaotic. You may have imagined a central command centre or headquarters, with various sub-stations or patrols and excellent communications and transport. On the other hand you may have imagined a pokey office with a sign on the door reading 'Out to lunch' or 'Back in two hours'; a permanently engaged, or out-of-order telephone line; or an answering service that places you in a queue and plays irritating music. You may make contact with the healing forces only to be told to call back later.

Your reaction to this kind of service may also be significant. Did you accept the situation, like Sheila who made no objection when she was rudely told to call her healing forces again in two weeks, or did you insist that they respond to your request for help immediately? When they did respond, Sheila's 'force' of firefighters were too fat to slide down their poles, had insufficient fire-engines, while those they had were in a poor state of repair. Your healing forces may have seemed no better than Sheila's, unable to defend the body against invasion and to maintain or restore its health. They may have been uncooperative, ignored or refused your request for help.

You may have found your healing forces willing and responsive but quite disorganised, like David's fire fighting force which travelled throughout his entire body before locating the fire in their own headquarters. Your healing forces may have been highly efficient and well organised – German panzer divisions, Ghurka regiments, closely coordinated special task forces, or colonies of ants. They may have been too efficient and needed to be restrained or retrained; or they may have appeared more efficient than they actually are, such as the cats Ann imagined removing the troublesome mice from her kitchen. Rather than killing them the cats were carrying the mice out of the house, alive, and placing them on a skip in the garden.

Your healing forces may have seemed badly depleted and unable to carry out the necessary work adequately or quickly enough.

## Possible results

While your imagery may be entertaining and amusing it is nevertheless a serious enterprise. It can be quite remarkably powerful in providing insights into your health and illness. It may provide some indication of your immune response, together with how this may be consciously influenced in support of treatment. It may also reveal your unconscious attitudes and expectations about health and illness. It may alleviate or remove completely chronic tensions and long-standing pains. It may highlight previously unrecognised connections between apparently discrete muscle groups and body parts which may have important implications for the management and treatment of certain painful conditions.

Visualisation may also bring about dramatic recovery.

## Immediate effects

Sometimes the effects of visualisation are immediate. The first time that Veronica tried it she regained full mobility in her knee, Justin successfully treated a severe throat infection at his first attempt and Michael overcame the lingering effects of glandular fever. You may find that your aches, pains and tensions are relieved after only one attempt, and that they do not return. Sore throats, coughs, headaches and migraine may disappear quickly. However, the effects may take more time. Christine, Lynn, Brenda and Jen all attribute the disappearance of lumps in a breast to regular visualisation over several weeks. Jean and Alex used visualisation successfully to avoid the unpleasant side-effects of the chemotherapy they received for breast cancer. Their experiences are by no means uncommon. Jack's long-standing tennis elbow responded to daily visualisation and disappeared after two weeks' practice.

## Other physical effects

Visualisation may also be effective in producing other physical effects. When Jane undertook the above exercise she felt great discomfort in her stomach. Following an illness a year previously which had reduced her mobility, she had gained over a stone in weight, mostly in her stomach region. When she imagined herself entering her body she saw herself standing on a vast area of smooth fat rather like an ice floe, with very little space overhead between it and her skin. As she tried to work out whether the fat could be cut through in some way, or part of it cut off, a white helicopter appeared overhead and a man in a white space-type suit with a personal radio in his hand descended from a rope to stand beside her. He explained that it was not possible to cut into the fat or remove it because of its blood supply. When Jane asked how it could be removed he replied that the only way was to melt it and this would require an increase in temperature. He then transported her to the operational headquarters of what appeared to be a very modern, fully computerised power station.

After examining the data presented on various monitors, he showed her a dial with a reading of 70. This, he explained was an indicator of her metabolic rate. He turned the dial so that it read 110, explaining as he did so that while this increase was substantial it was necessary to reduce the excess energy she had stored as fat. He also explained that she would not see an immediate effect because the increase in metabolic rate would build slowly and it would then take some time to act on the fat. Jane was impressed by his efficiency and confident that she would witness changes in her weight before long. Within a few weeks she had lost several pounds in weight.

# 8

## MANAGING
## PAIN

Visualisation can be used to relieve or remove pain in the same way as other symptoms of disease. Cathy suffered intermittently over a five-year period and persistently over four months from a painful hip. It had become so painful that for some weeks she had walked with a limp. Her condition had been diagnosed as arthritis stemming from her early career as a dancer, and unrelieved by medical treatment. The first time Cathy visualised her hip (after following the 'Communicating with your body processes' exercise in Chapter 7) she imagined a maintenance man in blue overalls examining a large white ball suspended in total darkness. He then took a large white file from his workbag and removed chalky-looking deposits that covered the ball. The next day she was pain-free for the first time in months.

When she repeated the exercise the same character appeared as a spaceman in a silver spacesuit. He focused several green lights on to her hip using a silver tray as a reflector. She realised the light was love, and took this to mean that she didn't love or care sufficiently for this part of her body, which she thought hardly surprising given the pain it caused her. The following day she could lift her leg fully.

When she next visualised her 'hip problem' she recognised it might be more than simply physical. She acknowledged that she feared losing the high-profile lifestyle she was accustomed to, and her 'hipness' among peers. She thought it was time to be less 'hip', decided to change her trendy hairstyle for something more conventional, and did so. Within a week of the first visualisation she was able to wear high heels for the first time in many months.

## How Visualisation Works On Pain

As Cathy's experience shows, both physical and psychological factors contribute to pain. Although we tend to think of pain as originating in our body, it is essentially something that occurs in our mind. Attention, memory, expectation, belief, imagination and learning are all involved in pain experience, even when there is a known physical cause. Pain can be increased if we are anxious because anxiety creates greater muscle tension which contributes to pain experience. Visualisation can reverse these effects by enabling us to relax.

Pain also increases if we focus our attention on it. If we are distracted from it, pain decreases. Visualisation alleviates pain by distracting our attention from it.

All the indications from both everyday experience and scientific research support the view that the opportunity to anticipate the effects of a 'painful' stimulus generally guarantees a 'painful' response which might not otherwise be experienced, or at least not to the same degree. If we believe that the source of the pain cannot be controlled the experience of pain seems to be inevitable. These are, of course, the basic principles of torture. Ironically it is also a feature of many medical practices which encourage the individual to focus on pain rather than distract attention from it. Health care professionals routinely advise that 'this might hurt' when administering injections or taking blood, thereby sensitising us to pain; and they also often 'programme' cancer patients to expect pain, discomfort, nausea and hair loss as 'normal' features of their treatment. Perhaps the most obvious and common abuse of the 'torture principle' comes in childbirth, where women are often encouraged to focus on 'the pains' rather than the pleasure, and therefore on negative rather than positive aspects of their experience.

If we believe that pain can be controlled we are likely to experience less pain and suffering than if we believe it cannot be controlled. The belief that pain can be controlled may have positive consequences even if in reality the pain is not controlled. What is important is the perception of control. You are likely to feel more positive if you believe you can control pain. This is usually sufficient to reduce the intensity, unpleasantness and discomfort of acute pain because it decreases uncertainty and anxiety. Where pain is chronic the belief that it can be controlled is all important to the degree of suffering experienced. The significant factor in treatment is not the actual technique used but whether the person believes it will be helpful and applicable. Enabling a patient to perceive control is therefore very important.

Health care professionals may inadvertently enhance the pain experience of chronic sufferers by stripping pain of its subjective and psychological dimensions and implying that it is something external to the person to be controlled by physicians and drugs rather than dealt with in a way that enables the person to take responsibility for it or to recognise its significance. By so doing they generate negative expectations which in turn increase anxiety and tension.

Psychological approaches to pain essentially employ these principles in reverse, to alleviate rather than enhance pain. They use methods that combine relaxation and visualisation to expose and modify the perceptions, beliefs and meanings we hold about pain. These methods therefore work with pain rather than against it, and confront rather than avoid it. By way of these images we can confront and communicate with pain directly and gain a sense of control over it. This helps to reduce our anxiety and to break the cycle of fear and tension that often builds up and overwhelms us if we suffer chronic pain. With our fear reduced it is easier for us to develop a more positive attitude, which in turn further reduces anxiety and tension, and as we relax and become more calm pain begins to recede from the forefront of our attention. With less of our energy taken up fighting pain and fears we can become stronger and invest more energy in our everyday life and its enjoyment. Even if you are suffering a terminal condition your quality of life can be improved greatly through visualisation.

Visualisation can therefore help to reduce pain in a number of ways, and to augment and reinforce other treatment approaches. It can also provide important insights into the nature of pain and the non-physical factors that contribute to it. Children spontaneously use imagery to describe their physical and emotional pain whereas adults do not. Unlike children, adults have to re-learn how to access their imagination and harness the results. The following exercise will enable you to do so. It is a highly effective way to gain relief from and insight into pain.

## EXERCISE 7

### Gaining an Insight into Pain

Relax as fully as possible in whatever way you find easiest. When you have done so, identify any areas of pain that remain in your body or those areas where pain tends to occur. Focus your attention on these areas, one at a time, and allow an image to form in response to the sensations you experience there. Try not to influence or censor this in any way. Simply receive what comes to mind. If nothing comes to mind don't try to produce an image, simply allow yourself to relax further while maintaining a passive focus on the area in question.

When an image forms, note its features, paying particular attention to its colour, shape and size, and what you can learn about your pain from this image. You may find that you can interact and communicate with it. If so ask it why it is there and what it is doing. Ask it also what it is doing for you, and what you can do for it.

When you have done so, try to change its colour, and as you do so notice any reactions you experience physically, mentally or emotionally. Then change its shape and size. Experiment with as many changes as you can and notice your physical, mental and emotional reactions as you do so.

When you have made as many changes as you can, shrink the pain and project it as far out of your body as you can, and until it is out of sight. If you wish to, allow the pain to reappear and to return to its former position in your body, noting as it does so any changes in sensation you experience. When you have done so, allow the image to fade, return to ordinary awareness and record your experience.

# Commentary

## *Pictures of pain*

Most people find it easier to describe pain in pictures than in words. This is particularly true of children who frequently describe physical and emotional pain in terms of imagery which all too frequently is dismissed by adults as nonsense. By doing so, or reassuring them that there have never been 'monsters in the dark' or 'alligators under the bed', or that they have gone away, adults often fail to recognise the significance of these images and deny children the opportunity of healing themselves. The importance of imagery in revealing the nature, significance and experience of pain is now becoming more widely recognised, and is increasingly being used in conjunction with other psychological methods in its assessment and management.

We have a very limited vocabulary for pain. This makes it difficult to express or convey it to others, which is why it is usually easier to draw pain. When asked to draw their pain adults and children typically use the colours black, red, orange or brown, and less commonly as purple or green. The more intense the pain the more likely they are to draw it as red or black. Drawings tend to be larger the more severe the pain is, and children typically depict acute pain as spikey abstract shapes that convey sensations of 'sharpness'. They usually depict less acute pain as more smooth, with curved rather than jagged outlines. Adults are less likely to draw abstract shapes than children and more likely to use words and phrases in their drawings.

## Changing the imagery

Many people discover that changing their imagery in various ways has striking and dramatic effects. Smoothing the edges of pain images can bring relief, as can changing its shape. Some people find that simply imagining the colour of the pain changing has immediate effects. Changing red and orange pains to blue or green can produce relief, especially if they are experienced as 'burning' sensations, or as 'raging'. Tension and migraine headaches respond well to blue, which generally appears to have a soothing effect when substituted for other colours. Sensations that appear as 'black and blue' respond well to red and orange, and where the colour of pain is vivid, diluting it can bring about marked improvement in reducing pain experience. Roger's painful throat problems disappeared once he began to change the red imagery associated with it to blue, and Shirley gained significant relief from her rheumatoid arthritis by changing her green pain imagery to orange. Experimentation with colour should reveal which is most appropriate to your particular pain. (For more information on colour, see my book *Healing With Colour*.)

Pain can also become less severe when it is imagined shrinking. You may be able to shrink it so that it disappears entirely, or project your pain so far from your body that you can no longer 'see' it, or feel it. You might suppose that in most cases the relief experienced is only short term and that the pain will return. Certainly if you expect the pain to return it probably will because this is tantamount to inviting it to do so. However, if you can achieve even fleeting relief from pain this may be sufficient to persuade you that you have some degree of control over your perception of pain and therefore your experience of it. With practice you may be able to develop this ability and extend the pain-free periods. Edith, who had received every conceivable treatment for pain relief without success, 'saw' her pain floating, 'disembodied' outside her but was unable to feel it. She felt confident that having discovered how to achieve this she could train herself to dissociate from the pain completely.

## Confronting the pain

While dissociating from pain has its undoubted uses in the management of severe and chronic pain, in most cases confronting the issue is considerably more beneficial than avoiding it. Pain researchers suggest that like hunger and thirst, pain is better classified as an awareness of need-state than as a sensation, and that it acts as a message that the body should initiate healing. Pain should therefore be attended to and confronted rather than avoided and ignored. However, because the nature of pain is difficult to convey verbally its meaning and significance frequently elude us. Visualisation not only enables us simply to view or gain a different perspective on pain but also to confront it directly. It allows us both to speak and listen to our pains and often provides insights that enable us to act on the message they communicate.

You may be reluctant to speak to your knee or neck, perhaps because as a child you were told that talking to yourself is the first sign of madness, and so you consider it a crazy idea. What is more crazy is that most of us don't regard our bodies as part of ourselves in the same way as our minds. This is merely a convention. Whereas in the West we view the brain as the seat of intelligence, the Japanese traditionally locate it in the stomach. As a result we consider intelligence as confined to the brain rather than distributed through our whole body, and don't avail itself of its wisdom. Hence we don't listen to our bodies. However, if and when we do, we may be astonished by the information it conveys. When David asked his back why it hurt it told him he didn't want to go back to work. As a result he was obliged to confront work-related problems he had previously tried to repress. Jill's painful ankles told her she would not be able to 'stand firm' through her forthcoming and unwanted divorce.

You might think it strange that the exercise allows you to restore your pain to its original site. You may suppose that people would be pleased to rid themselves of it and would not want it back. This is certainly true for some people, like Edith, but for many the idea of their pain disappearing completely produces anxiety. Closer examination usually reveals that pain fulfils an important function in their life. It may be a conversation piece or a way of gaining the attention of others; or it may relieve them of unpleasant and unwanted roles, duties, responsibilities and obligations. If you find that you are reluctant or unable to let your pain disappear entirely, ask it what function it serves in your life – what it does for you – and whether it is possible for you to meet this need in another, less painful way.

## Pain images

Confronting pain directly by speaking to it may be easier when the shape it assumes is not abstract. You may find that your pain images take the shape of persons known to you, such as a relative or spouse. Joan identified her 'pain in the neck' as her dependent mother, and Sheila described the pain in her chest as her mother lying along the length of her collar bone. Mothers and mothers-in-law are frequently 'seen' as pains in the neck, chest and back, usually by those women with the task of looking after them. It is perhaps not surprising that people perceived as burdens produce pains in those who see them in that way.

Daughters are also often described as 'pains', and most commonly located in the chest. Mary, who describes herself as 'stifled' by her daughter, experiences chest pains and breathing difficulties in her presence. Dorothy associates her angina with visits from her married daughter. These physical pains may be the only way these women can express their ambivalent or hostile attitudes to their children. It is not the 'done thing' for mothers to express dislike of their children, and so they often find it difficult to admit, even to themselves, the 'heartache' they experience in their relationships with them.

This may also be true of those people, like Margaret, who, because of religious beliefs opposed to divorce, cannot admit to profoundly unhappy marriages. When men experience similar difficulties they seem to develop pains in their lower back, buttocks and bowels, suggesting perhaps that they tend to suppress these feelings by 'sitting on them'.

Visualisation may enable you to confront your painful relationships and to express your feelings to hurtful people in ways that might be difficult or impossible for you to do otherwise. It may be that the person to whom your feelings are directed is dead. Imagining a direct encounter with them can complete 'unfinished business' and allow healing to take place.

## *Pain and loss*

You may find yourself confronting deep emotional hurt when you focus on your physical pains, like Caroline who said, 'Every time I focus on my physical pains I find that it is actually my feelings that are hurt'. Typically loss of some kind is discovered; of a baby or child, relationship or marriage, a job, status or self-respect, or loss of a loved one. Invariably the initial hurt has been covered up, often much too quickly, rather than exposed and aired. Irritants may have also been sealed in and buried just as when a sticking-plaster is too hastily applied, so on the surface the issue appears to have been dealt with but real healing has not taken place. In some cases the wound has continued to fester beneath the skin, sometimes producing problems out of all proportion to the original hurt. These may erupt much later and not be recognised as having any connection with the initial trauma, or they may simply poison the whole system.

You may have grieved for a loss, but only cursorily, so that it appears to have been dealt with, but your anger about it may not have been expressed. This undischarged anger may have festered as resentment, which is always unhealthy, unlike anger which is neutral and only positive or negative depending on how it is expressed. Resentment usually develops because feelings are not aired and it often proves deadly because it is associated with various serious diseases, including cancer. Hasty cover-ups of normal, healthy emotions often leads to malignancy, and the process is all too frequently assisted by the medical practice of prescribing tranquillisers and anti-depressants to those experiencing loss or bereavement.

## Express your feelings

If you have never aired your feelings you may not have identified them appropriately. You may assume that you are sad when in fact you are intensely angry. Marjorie was shocked to hear herself saying about her son who had died tragically in an accident, 'If he were alive now I'd kill him'. When she examined her feelings more closely she realised she felt angry, not only because her son had died pursuing a dangerous hobby she had always disapproved of, but also because his death had prevented her from realising her ambitions. Cynthia admitted she was 'consumed' with resentment towards the car driver who had survived the crash in which her son was killed.

Whatever the initial trauma, anger invariably occurs when we experience loss. If not expressed it will continue to eat away at us unless or until we allow it to surface. These hurt feelings must be dealt with and treated with as much respect as physical tissue damage. Failure to do so may result in far greater pain. Visualisation provides a most important means of dealing with these issues, which are often difficult to access and express verbally, not only because society doesn't encourage their expression but also because by their very nature they are non-verbal, emotional and easily repressed. Visualisation 'puts us in the picture' about these hidden, unconscious feelings and obliges us to 'face up' to them.

## Distraction from pain

You may think that dissociating from pain and relieving it by way of visualisation runs counter to the idea that pain is a warning message which should be listened to and acted upon. However, as a result of psychological factors pain can not only be more perceptible but can become entirely disproportionate to the degree of actual tissue damage. It can also persist long after injured tissue has healed. Rather like a broken car horn it may not be blaring any useful warning. An alternative to 'turning off' the horn is to distract attention away from it. Most people, however, become obsessed with pain, often to the extent that it distracts from everything else.

This is particularly true of those people who suffer from tinnitus, a condition where persistent ringing, hissing or booming occurs in one or both ears. Although not physically painful it creates tremendous psychological distress, and is often described as 'agony' or 'torture' by sufferers. Many of those so afflicted are unable to relax or sleep because of the incessant noise. As a result their tension and distress escalates and their attention becomes increasingly focused on the problem that threatens to overwhelm them. Bill was on the verge of a nervous breakdown following the onset of tinnitus, which had resulted in the loss of his job and many ordinary pleasures including reading. After attempting visualisation only six times he was able to read for lengthy periods and was able to resume a more normal life.

# 9

## FINDING YOUR HIGHER SELF

There is a widespread belief in most cultures that we are more than the sum of our physical and psychological parts, and that each of us has an immaterial, eternal, spiritual aspect or soul which functions beyond our conscious awareness to give shape and structure to our lives, influencing, directing and regulating it. Although its processes are to a great extent unknown to the conscious mind, the soul communicates by way of feelings, intuitions, dreams and images.

## The Spiritual In The Material World

In primitive societies the soul was, and still is, perceived as permeating air, earth and water and all the diverse forms assumed by persons, animals, plants and objects. The spiritual and the sacred are not divorced from the natural world and the material body, therefore, because the material world is impregnated with spiritual qualities.

This all-pervading quality unifies humanity and nature, and the present with the eternal because it is integral to an infinite and eternal universe in which no part is separate from any other. The spirit realm therefore permeates all time and space and endows the world with life and meaning. The aim and purpose of life is to maintain contact with the soul, which is the core or essence of each person, the true self. Losing sight of the soul is disastrous as it renders life pointless and meaningless.

The idea of this spirit or soul as the vehicle of personal existence can be traced within Western civilisation from antiquity to the present day. It has been the subject of poetry and philosophy, but is chiefly the province of religion. In the ancient world all human problems were seen as spiritual in origin. They were the result of losing sight of or touch with soul, essence or psyche – the true self. Physical disorders were considered symptomatic of this fundamental dis-ease, and all treatment was concerned with the cure of the soul – the literal meaning of the word psychotherapy – restoring contact with it and making the person whole again. This idea is found in the terms *health* and *healing* which are closely allied to words meaning whole and holy. Literally, therefore, to be healthy is to be whole or holy. Health clearly embraces both the physical and spiritual aspects of being. Religion and medicine therefore developed together in almost all cultures.

However from the seventeenth century onwards religion and medicine became separated as science developed an almost exclusively materialistic emphasis. Inevitably Western culture began to lose sight of the soul. However, a New Age has become progressively disillusioned with materialism. As a result in the late twentieth century there has been a resurgence of interest in spirituality and a growing recognition of its importance to health.

# 'The Divine In You'

The New Age has provided a new adage. What has been known to humanity down the ages as the spirit or soul is now widely referred to as the Higher Self. One of best-known exponents of the New Age, Shirley MacLaine explains that the 'Higher Self is exactly what the words imply – the best positive elements of your own being, the most reassuring aspect of your own inner strength, your personal expression of the Divine in you. It links with everything else that exists: it is your channel to the enormous resources of the human potential' (see Bibliography). She points out that it is an aspect of yourself with which you can have an actual discussion about whatever is troubling you. 'Connecting with your Higher Self is what enables you to see within, and listening to its guidance can provide you with direction in every aspect of your life'. Not surprisingly, establishing or re-establishing contact with it has for many people become a priority.

You may wonder how this is achieved. For most people it amounts to regaining sight of their soul, but it can be perceived in many ways. Some people hear it as a voice within. Others sense it as feeling. Many people see it as form. People have viewed their Higher Selves as persons, animals, shapes of light, geometric designs and so on but irrespective of how it is perceived the experience is invariably very profound.

*Coming into alignment with my Higher Self caused an expanded self-awareness in me, which automatically led to an expanded awareness and a gentler understanding of others. At the same time, touching my Higher Self created a sense of being aligned with the universal spirit, so that I felt a keener*

*understanding of the concept that we are all one.
Bridging this gap may be the most important
connection I've made in life because it enables me to
feel empowered and to transform my perception of the
outside world I have chosen to live in. By expanding
my perception of self, I stop feeling so helpless and
victimized and realise with full profundity that I can
transform anything I want by transforming myself.
That transformation begins within.*

Shirley MacLaine, *Going Within*

Transformation of the self begins with insight, with looking inwards. It came about for Shirley MacLaine by allowing pictures to unfold in her mind. 'It was,' she says 'like watching a series of excerpts from long-forgotten films unspool in the theatre of my mind'. When she questioned the logic of the pictures she imagined, they disappeared, so she allowed the pictures to unravel without judgement. In other words, her transformation came about through visualisation.

For many people spiritual growth and development have occurred as a consequence of visions of many kinds. In some cases these have occurred spontaneously but in many more cases they have resulted from intentional visualisation. The following exercise will provide spiritual insights by helping you to make contact with your Higher Self, spirit or soul.

## EXERCISE 8

### Contacting Your Higher Self

**Imagine a warm sunny day and that you are
walking in the countryside. You walk until you**

see a cave. In the mouth of the cave you see a large rock. You go into the cave and sit on the rock in order to cool down.

Looking around you see a lamp further inside the cave. You walk over to it and, remembering the story of Aladdin, pick it up and begin to rub it. Suddenly a genie emerges from the lamp and, still thinking about Aladdin, you find yourself saying out loud 'Your wish is my command'. Observe the genie carefully, noting every aspect of its appearance and manner and your feelings towards it. Pay careful notice to any message it communicates in whatever way, and how you respond to it.

Having done so, allow the image to fade. Return to normal awareness and take some time to record your experience.

# Commentary

The word genie, which refers to a magical presence that fulfils wishes, derives from a Latin word meaning 'attendant spirit'. It is similar in origin to the word genius, which refers to exceptional ability. These different meanings are all reflected in responses to the above exercise. You may suppose that everyone would welcome the opportunity to perceive their personal genius and to realise their highest potentials. This is not so.

## The unwelcome genie

Some people don't want to see the genie. They want to leave it where it is. Closer examination suggests that they don't want to acknowledge their potential because they

don't want to take responsibility for it and its consequences. Their reasoning is often that if they knew what
they are capable of they would have no excuse for failure;
or, more specifically, no excuse for not even trying to
realise their potentials. If despite their resistance they do
see the genie they may try and trap it in the lamp or push
it back in, reflecting their desire to deny and repress this
aspect of themselves. Your responses to the exercise may
therefore enable you to identify anxieties and fears that
prevent you from listening to your Higher Self and bene-
fiting from its guidance and advice.

Many people are shocked or frightened by the sheer
size of the genie because invariably it is huge. They may
try to reduce its size in various ways. Julie described
shrinking her genie 'to bring him down to size'. In so
doing she realised that she always has low aspirations
because she thinks 'things will be too much for her' and
so is always trying to bring things down to what she
perceives as her level. Kath also shrank her huge turbaned
genie so that he was able to stand in the palm of her hand.
He responded to her statement 'Your wish is my
command' by saying that he wanted to be bigger. She did
as he requested and increased him from matchstick size to
about 30 cm in height. She would not let him get bigger.
She realised that she wanted him to remain 'in the palm of
her hand', in her control, and that he represented her
potential, or genius. She feared that if he grew more she
would lose control, and recognised this as a central
dilemma of her life – wanting to develop her potentials
but always acting to prevent this occurring. When she
examined this more closely she acknowledged this self-
limiting strategy as a way of maintaining the status quo
and not having to take responsibility for change in her
life.

Jackie felt angry when she imagined herself saying 'Your wish is my command' because she felt that the genie should have said this to her, and that, unlike other people whose genies appeared to them, she would not get her wish fulfilled. She wanted the genie to work for her rather than she for him. Reluctantly she acknowledged that much of her energy is used in envying the success of others whom she sees as having 'got on' without effort, rather than making an effort to succeed herself.

## Positive reactions

Other people experience peace, calm, warmth, love, support or enlightenment when they see their genie, or intense spiritual feelings. Wendy was unable to see any genie at all but had a powerful sensation of being held, supported and loved. The genie may not speak but by its actions may communicate profound messages and insights. In many cases the genie signifies a desire for contact by outstretching its arms, or proferring a hand. David felt a profound sense of one-ness with nature when his genie touched him. Until her genie touched her, Christine had been more interested in the huge ruby in his turban than in him. She then realised that he was worth far more to her than jewels because he was her higher soul principle.

Clearly for many people the genie they see is influenced by children's storybook or pantomime images of a large, rotund, sallow-skinned exotically dressed man, wearing a jewelled turban. Others image a very different genie. To some he looks like Christ. Ursula felt in awe of the Jesus-like character she imagined. He had no feet and did not touch the ground, so seemed to her to be 'hanging around'. Then he reached down and drew her up to his level, and as she received 'this helping hand' she realised he was her guardian angel. Many people encounter their guardian angel in this way, although it might not be for the first time. Cathy recognised the genie as the guardian angel whose presence she had sensed throughout her life but had never previously communicated with. In this encounter he spoke and she listened to his advice and guidance for the first time. Dan's guardian angel 'showed him the light' by projecting visions on to the cave wall which gave him profound insights into himself and the universe and changed his outlook on life entirely. Yvonne's genie showed her a candle, and as she received it she 'saw the light' and felt as though her prayers had been answered. She realised that this light 'meant the world' to her.

These experiences, which are by no means uncommon, echo the wisdom of Kahlil Gibran's prophet:

*No man can reveal to you aught but that which*
*already lies half asleep in the dawning of your*
*knowledge ... For the vision of one man lends not its*
*wings to another man.*

*And even as each one of you stands alone in God's*
*knowledge, so must each one of you be alone in his*
*knowledge of God and in his understanding of the*
*earth.*

# BIBLIOGRAPHY AND FURTHER READING

Gibran, K. (1991) *The Prophet*, London: Pan Books.

Graham, H. (1990) *Time, Energy and the Psychology of Healing*, London: Jessica Kingsley.

Graham, H. (1992) *The Magic Shop: An imaginative guide to self healing*, London: Rider.

Graham, H. (1995) *Mental Imagery in Health Care: An introduction to therapeutic practice*, London: Chapman and Hall.

Graham, H. (1995) *A Picture of Health: Using guided imagery for personal growth and self-healing*, London: Piatkus.

Graham, H. (1996) *Healing With Colour*, Dublin: Gill and Macmillan.

Hemery, D. (1978) Interviewed by Sir John Whitmore *New Life Magazine*, p. 23, Autumn 21–5.

Le Carré, J. (1989) *The Russia House*, p. 122, London: Hodder & Stoughton.

Levine, B.H. (1991) *Your Body Believes Everything You Say: The language of body/mind connection*, Boulder Creek CA: Aslan Publishing.

MacLaine, S. (1989) *Going Within: A guide for inner transformation*, p. 67, London: Transworld Publishers.

Morgan, G. (1993) *Imaginization: The art of creative management*, p. 12, London: Sage.

Seigel, B.S. (1986) *Love, Medicine and Miracles*, London: Rider.

Simonton, O.C., Matthews-Simonton, S. & Creighton, J. (1978) *Getting Well Again*, New York: Bantam.

# INDEX